SUNDAY DINNER

SUNDAY DINNER

*The Lord's Supper and the
Christian Life*

William H. Willimon

THE UPPER ROOM
Nashville, Tennessee

Sunday Dinner

The scripture quotations not otherwise identified are from the Revised Standard Version of the Bible, copyrighted 1946, 1952 and © 1971 by the Division of Christian Education, National Council of Churches of Christ in the United States of America, and are used by permission.

The initials KJV are used throughout this book to identify quotations from the King James Version of the Bible.

Interior and cover illustrations by Bruce Sayre
Book design: Harriette Bateman
First printing: October, 1981 (8)
Second Printing: November, 1982 (7)
Library of Congress Catalog Card Number: 81-52215
ISBN 0-8358-0429-1
Printed in the United States of America

To my mother

Contents

Introduction: Sunday Dinner

If you're like me, some of your earliest and fondest childhood memories are memories of family meals. I particularly remember Sunday dinner. Sunday dinner took place at my grandfather's big, rambling house where we all gathered after church. *Family* meant more than mother, father, brothers, and sisters. *Family* meant that entire army of cousins, aunts, uncles—including an occasional passerby whose relationship to the clan was less clear. Uncles gathered in the living room for cigars and arguments. Aunts assembled in the kitchen for the preparation of dinner and arguments. Cousins chased each other up and down my grandmother's big front porch, oblivious to our parents' periodic pleas to be careful with our Sunday clothes and our cousins' skulls.

By mid-afternoon, all were complaining of famine. You had to wait for Sunday dinner, wait well into late afternoon before it commenced. But at last it came and it was worth the wait. We all gathered at the long, dining-room table, seated through directives from my grandmother, who always had firmly fixed in her mind exactly where everyone was to sit: mama was at one end; papa was presiding over the ritual at the other end; aunts, uncles, and cousins were fixed at their appointed stations between.

The meal began with a seemingly interminable prayer by papa. Then, all having been blessed, there was the raucous, joyful falling upon the feast. This was followed by a period of silence broken only by the tinkling of knives and forks. Then the table talk began. Cousins listened while aunts and uncles argued over the next county election and thoroughly discussed all matters of importance. When the elders spoke, all listened in attentive deference to the wisdom of the ages. Occasionally, some teenaged upstart of a cousin would offer an ill-considered opinion on the matter under discussion only to be hooted down by aunts and uncles or else patiently instructed in correct opinions by papa or mama. There were always stories, lots of stories about family exploits of the past, stories about heroes, funny stories, our stories.

This was our family's Sunday ritual. As we grew older and had families of our own, more cousins for the clan, we took our places among the elders, moving up along the side of the dinner table, one seat closer to the chiefs of the tribe.

Because of this Sunday mealtime ritual, no one had to tell me what it meant to be a part of this family. No one had to tell me who I was or instruct me in the proper world view for folk with our name. I never got formal instruction in orthodox belief or behavior. No one had to explain to me that I belonged or that I was loved. I learned all that at the Sunday dinner table. If someone had asked me, "Who are your people and what do they stand for?" I would have responded quite honestly, "My people are those who gather at grandmother's dinner table." At the table we were initiated, nurtured, and claimed into the family. There we participated in common memory, fellowship, and identity. There we found our place, our name, our story—at the table.

Remember Who You Are: Baptism, A Model for Christian Life spoke of baptism as the beginning of a Christian's pilgrimage. *Sunday Dinner* is a book about how people are best nurtured and sustained in the Christian journey. It is a book about the Lord's Supper; it is a book about meals. It is written from the conviction that in a Christian's participation in the Lord's Supper, we see the principal place of a Christian's identity, sustenance, conversion, and growth.

This book seeks to demonstrate that the bread and wine of the Lord's Supper are the normal food for Christians. It arises out of the biblical affirmation that the Lord's Supper is the normal Sunday dinner of the family of God which we call the church.

This is a book for those who want to explore the meaning of the gift of the Lord's Supper and its significance for their daily lives as Christians. The Lord's Supper is a rich experience, too rich for mere words. We speak of it by many names, each illuminating a different aspect of this holy meal. We call it the Lord's Supper, reminding ourselves of that primal experience of table fellowship which was enjoyed by Jesus and his disciples and continued in the church. We call it Holy Communion, reminding ourselves than in this eating and drinking together we are in the presence of Christ and our brothers and sisters in Christ. We call it the Eucharist, coming from the Greek word *Eucharistein,* meaning "to give thanks." This reminds us that the Lord's Supper is an act of joy and thankfulness for the work of God in Jesus Christ. We have also called this meal the Mass. This designation comes from the words at the end of the Lord's Supper as it was celebrated in the medieval church, "You are sent out," (*Ite Missa Est*). In the Mass, Christians receive the nourishment and sustenance they need in order to go out into the world to do the work that they are supposed to do. Like the different facets of a brilliant diamond, each of these names—the Lord's Supper, Holy Communion, Eucharist, the Mass—helps us to see some aspect of this meal in a new light.

Each of these names also reminds us of what a rich and varied experience we are discussing in this book. We cannot say everything that could be said about this experience, nor should we try. The command of Jesus is, "Take, eat," not, "Take, understand." At times our church has been guilty of giving people mere explanations about God when what they want most is an experience of God. Take this book as an invitation to new experiences with the presence of God in your life and in our world. Take this as bread for the journey. Thanks go to my parishioners at Northside United Methodist Church, my students at Duke Divinity School, and friends who first heard and responded to these thoughts as they developed. Thanks go also to Bruce Sayre for the illustrations and to John Westerhoff for the study guide.

And thanks go to all those fellow Christians who first invited me to the table, who showed me that my hungers need not go unfulfilled, who gave me bread and wine for the trip through the desert, who told me unforgettable stories around the table, and who endured my bad table manners—all so that someday I might know what to do and how to act when the Lord invited me to feast at his table forever.

In all those Sunday dinners, family night suppers, Lord's Suppers, church picnics, pancake breakfasts, barbecues, and all the rest, I learned how close our God is to us.

WILL WILLIMON
Good Friday, 1980

The Antioch Chalice
—6th century

CHAPTER ONE

Memories of Meals

They beheld God, and ate and drank.
—Exodus 24:11*b*

Stories at the Table

One of the things which people do at the dinner table is tell stories. They tell stories not simply to give themselves something to do while they eat, but because stories are important parts of the communion, fellowship, love, joy, and remembrance which make up the mystery of a meal. That is one of the reasons there are many stories in this book. When Christians eat together, especially when they eat together in the Lord's Supper, part of the serious and joyful business of being at the table is storytelling. Just as Jesus told stories to his disciples when they ate together, so we tell stories. These stories tell us who we are, why we are together, and what the table is preparing us for.

Recently I ate with a group of old friends at a Chinese restaurant. Most of them were high school friends that I had not seen for fifteen years or more. We had spread to the four corners of the world, but we were back together for a reunion. As is often the case on such occasions, after the food was served and the dinner table conversation had begun, our talk turned into storytelling. One by one, we told stories of past events, funny memories of evenings spent together. Before long these ten virtual strangers were close friends once again, brought together by memories and stories and laughter and communion around the table. That's often the way it is with stories—they remind us where we have come from and where we are and where we are going.

Jewish Meals and Stories

In the Jewish Passover feast, after the table is prepared and all is ready for the meal, a child asks the elders, "Why is this night special above all other nights?"—Why is this meal significant above other meals in the family?

The father replies by telling the ancient story of Israel's deliverance in the traditional Passover *Seder:*

> We were Pharaoh's slaves in Egypt, and the Lord our God brought us forth from there with a mighty and an outstretched arm. And if the Holy One, blessed be he, had not brought our forefathers forth from Egypt, then we, our children, and our children's children would still be Pharaoh's slaves in Egypt. . . . And the more one tells the story of the departure from Egypt, the more praiseworthy he is.

This Passover meal with the bitter herbs (remembering the bitterness of slavery and the sojourn in the wilderness) and unleavened bread (remembering the flight out of Egypt before the bread had time to rise) and lamb (which is eaten in haste, as if eaten by fugitives on the run from an enemy) is a meal in celebration and commemoration of the Exodus from Egypt. The dinner table is a place to tell the story.

But the story is not just historical recollection of some past event. The story is told as a present enactment of salvation. In telling the story, in eating the meal, past becomes present; the present generation become active participants in the Exodus:

> In every generation let each man look on himself
> as if he came forth from Egypt.
> As it is said: "And thou shalt tell thy son in
> that day, saying: It is because of that which
> the Lord did for me when I came forth from Egypt."

In the Passover meal and its table talk and stories, present-day Jews remember not only who they *were* but who they *are.* For the Jew, the Passover meal is an occasion for remembering and enacting what it means to be one of God's chosen people now.

When Christians eat the Lord's Supper, we also might ask, "Why is this meal special above other meals in our family?" One way of answering that question is to tell some stories of meals in our past.

The Bible begins our story with the eating of an apple and ends at the marriage supper of the Lamb. In the Old Testament, food, eating, and drinking are more significant in the faith of Israel than may appear at first glance. Even today, the Jewish people celebrate their holy days with feasts. We have already noted the Passover meal, the feast which celebrates the "passover" from Egypt slavery to freedom. In a sense, for the Jew *every* meal is a sacred occasion.

Our custom of saying a blessing or grace before meals comes from the Jews. In beginning a meal with prayer, in blessing food, the Jew claims food as a gift of God and the meal itself as a sacred occasion to come close to God through the gift of food and the gift of fellowship around the table. "God is great, God is good, let us thank him for this food" is a very Jewish prayer.

The greatness and goodness of God are manifested in many ways. Blessings before meals remind us that one of the most accessible, constant, everyday ways God's goodness and greatness are experienced is in the everyday gift of food and drink. The family dinner table becomes a place of divine-human meeting. The family meal becomes a kind of sacrament. We remind ourselves that God meets us in everyday life in such ordinary ways—ordinary bread, ordinary wine, ordinary people, ordinary conversation.

Because of the sacredness of meals, our ancestors in the faith saw meals and food as appropriate ways of being with God, as a means of celebrating the mystery of God's presence. When Noah and his family are delivered from the devastating flood, Noah celebrates their deliverance by making a thanksgiving offering to God (Gen. 8:20-22). The offering becomes an occasion for God to bless Noah and to make a promise or covenant with humanity. God says,

> This is the sign of the covenant which I make between me and you
> and every living creature that is with you, for all future generations.
> . . . the waters shall never again become a flood to destroy all flesh.
> —Genesis 9:12, 15*b*

Today when we give testimonial dinners to show our appreciation for someone, we are reflecting the thanksgiving sacrifices of the ancients. When we ratify international treaties and agreements with formal state dinners, we are continuing the ancient practice of sealing important contracts and covenants with a meal.

Few of us need be told that a meal is a sign of hospitality and friendship. Any child knows that when you share your candy bar with the new kid on the block, it is an act which produces instant friendship. In your family, when your daughter has been dating a young man and announces that she would like to bring him home for dinner, you sense that their relationship has moved to a more intimate and serious level. She is inviting this stranger into her family's inner sanctuary, to the family dinner table. You are correct in assuming that this signals something important may be about to happen.

The Old Testament knows this same connotation of meals with hospitality and friendship. Abraham receives three strangers into his home, prepares a fine feast for them, and is blessed for his hospitality (Gen. 18:1-16). Israel is often told to show hospitality to the "sojourner" and the "stranger within your gates."

In the twenty-third psalm, the psalmist joyfully sings, "Thou preparest a table before me in the presence of my enemies" (Psalm 23:5a). The psalmist sings of this act of hospitality as an act of great friendship. The person who invites you to dinner is the person who will stick beside you through thick and thin. This is especially true in the culture of the Near East, where meals and invitations to meals have even more significance than they do in our society. There, to be admitted to someone's table is a sign of lifelong devotion and undying loyalty.

I once heard a story about a nomad being pursued across the desert by his enemies. The desperate man comes upon an encampment. He rushes up to the tents, hoping that these strangers will receive him. He runs up to the head tent and throws back the curtains. The inhabitants have just begun to eat. Breathlessly he looks into their faces. Will they receive him or turn him away? They motion for him to enter and be seated. He breathes a sigh of relief. His pursuers finally reach the camp. They go to the tent he has entered. They also throw back the curtains, ready to seize the man and kill him. But when they see him seated at the table, they draw back and leave him in peace, for they know that in the Near East it is a great act of hostility toward the host to trouble a person who is seated at someone's table.

And so the psalmist says of God,

> The Lord is my shepherd, I shall not want. . . .
> Even though I walk through the valley of the shadow of death,

> I fear no evil;
>   for thou art with me;
>   thy rod and thy staff,
>   they comfort me.
>
> Thou preparest a table before me
>   in the presence of my enemies.
>   —Psalm 23:1, 4-5a

Just as an invitation to someone's table is the supreme sign of human hospitality, so is it seen as the supreme sign of God's hospitality to us.

The psalmist speaks of God preparing a table for us in the presence of our enemies. The prophet Isaiah, when he sees the final deliverance and salvation of Israel, picks up this theme of the invitation to the table. When the Messiah comes, the Messiah will invite all the wretched and the poor of Israel to come and eat without having to pay:

> Ho, every one who thirsts,
>   come to the waters;
> and he who has no money
>   come, buy and eat!
> Come, buy wine and milk
>   without money and without price.
>   —Isaiah 55:1

When this great day of deliverance comes and the messianic banquet is spread, even the Gentiles, even those who are not among God's chosen people, will be brought to the Lord.

> Behold, you shall call nations
>   that you know not,
>   and nations that knew you not
>   shall run to you,
> because of the Lord your God,
>   and of the Holy One of Israel,
>   for he has glorified you.
>   —Isaiah 55:5

For Israel, to look forward to the arrival of the Messiah meant to look forward to that day when God's Anointed One would come and invite all the poor and hungry to a great feast, a feast which would, according to Isaiah, eventually include even "nations that you know not."

As noted above, meals were often used to seal important agreements or covenants. The meal becomes a ratification of the covenant. In the account of the Last Supper which Jesus ate with his disciples in the upper room, Jesus quotes Exodus 24:8, "Behold the blood of the covenant which the Lord has made with you." These words come from the account of the feast of the covenant on Mt. Sinai (Exod. 24:1-11). In that ancient story, Moses goes up Sinai with Aaron, Nadab, Abihu, and seventy elders of Israel. On the mountain, the Lord yokes himself in love to Israel. Israel is to serve this God and this God alone. After the covenant with God is completed, the meeting ends with these extraordinary words, "They beheld God, and ate and drank" (Exod. 24:11b). The meal is seal for the covenant. The nation was God's guest; it sat at God's table.

Jeremiah foretold a day when the Lord would make a new covenant with Israel, because Israel broke the Sinai covenant many times with its waywardness and infidelity. In the new covenant, the Lord says,

> I will put my law within them, and I will write it upon their hearts; and I will be their God, and they shall be my people. . . . I will forgive their iniquity, and I will remember their sin no more.
> —Jeremiah 31:33, 34b

Previously a covenant had been akin to a contract: two parties had been bound to one another through an agreement to fulfill certain obligations. This new covenant of which Jeremiah speaks is hardly a covenant at all in the traditional sense of the word. Here is a unique relationship in which God unilaterally binds himself to Israel—not on the basis of what Israel can do for God, but solely on the basis of God's love for Israel.

At the end of his earthly ministry, Jesus gathers with his disciples one evening in the upper room for the Last Supper, takes the cup of wine, gives a prayer of thanks for it, and gives it to his disciples with the words, "This is my blood of the covenant, which is poured out for many" (Mark 14:24). We hear an echo of the ancient meal of Sinai which ratified the first covenant.

Looking back upon that meal in the upper room, Jesus' disciples would come to believe that since the cup was blessed and given by Jesus, it could be said of them, "They beheld God, and ate and drank."

Deliverance from slavery to freedom, a feast of joyful celebration and commemoration, an offering of thanksgiving, a sign of divine hospitality and friendship, the banquet of the Messiah, the seal of a new covenant—all of these earlier, older, mealtime memories are evident in that upper room meal. When Christ invited his disciples to the table, when he blessed the food, broke the bread, and shared the bread and the cup, the meal became a vivid, visible sign of God saying to the first Christians, "I will be their God, and they shall be my people" (Jer. 31:33).

The covenant was not broken in Jesus' death upon the cross; it was thereby ratified. Within days, his followers went forth joyfully preaching about his resurrection from the dead and how he had become "known to them in the breaking of the bread" at Emmaus (Luke 24:35). The presence, the joy, the love, the meals continued, even as they had during Jesus' earthly ministry. The followers of Christ not only taught, healed, preached, baptized, suffered, witnessed, believed, shared, and prayed— they also ate together. They shared in "the breaking of the bread."

> And they devoted themselves to the apostles' teaching and fellow-ship, to the breaking of bread and the prayers.
>
> —Acts 2:42

A Meal from Our Past

It is Sunday evening, the day when the business life of Jerusalem resumes after the Sabbath holiday. With the sun sinking from the sky, the narrow streets are emptying. Shopkeepers put in their wares, workmen mingle on one corner, a farmer coaxes a donkey out of a stall and toward home.[1]

Down one narrow passageway at the bottom floor of a warehouse, if you look closely, you can see men and women entering a small door toward the rear of the building. They are a mixed lot—old and young; an occasional Roman slave; a Jewish couple of some means; an old man who is obviously a shepherd from outside the city walls; a younger man who, judging from his dress, must be employed in the civil service; two younger women with their faces covered. Their lamps flicker and disappear in the entryway. Why are they gathering? What secret rite or shady business deal brings this motley group together?

They are being examined closely at the door as they enter. Whatever they are being questioned about must have nothing to do with their race or economic position or class, for one can plainly see that none of these factors unite them.

We enter, walking into a large room where a group of thirty or forty congregate around a simple wooden table. A man is reading from a scroll, the writings of one of the Hebrew prophets, it seems. His face is illuminated by two small lamps. The people listen intently until he is finished. He rolls up the scroll and steps to the rear of the group. An old man, one who is obviously venerated by the congregation, steps forward into the light and begins to speak. In his sermon, he exhorts the assembly to fulfill in their lives what they have heard in the sacred writings.

When the old man is finished, psalms are chanted; then all raise their hands and with their eyes open and hands outstretched toward heaven they pray, one by one offering simple spoken prayers for others. Someone of their group has been executed for failure to bow to the emperor; they pray for her. Others are in jail, awaiting trial; they pray for them. Sickness, persecution, poverty, the birth of a child—all are mentioned in their petitions. The prayer ends with a loud amen by all. They embrace each other in what they call the "kiss of peace" to seal the prayer and to prepare themselves for the evening meal.

Now, those called *deacons* (meaning "butler," "waiter," "servant") move among the congregation and collect bottles of wine and little loaves of bread which the people have brought with them. The food is gathered and placed upon the table. The aroma of fresh bread and new wine drifts over the assembly. The *bishop* (meaning "overseer"), as they call the old man, offers a prayer of thanksgiving, standing behind the table with his arms outstretched over the offering. In his prayer, he gives thanks for the work of God in the creation of the world, in God's love for Israel, and in Jesus Christ. He recalls Christ's meal with his disciples in the upper room, how Christ had broken bread and had given the bread and the cup to his disciples with the words, "Do this in remembrance of me."

The prayer ends with all saying a loud amen.

Each person is now given a large piece of the blessed bread and each takes a turn sipping from a large cup of wine. After everyone has eaten, the deacons collect the leftover bread and wine. Leftovers will be taken by the deacons to orphans and widows in the congregation. With the recent persecutions, there are many of them to be fed. Any who are sick or in need will also receive from the offering. "The rich among us come to the aid of the poor, and we always stay together," comments the bishop as the deacons wrap the food in a linen cloth and clean the crumbs away.

The bishop then raises his hands over the people and blesses them. They go forth, slipping out into the now deserted streets of the city. Their footsteps are heard sounding down the stone streets; then all is silent.

They have been fed. They have been nourished. They have been with their Lord. And now they are ready to return to the world. They slip out the door into the darkness, each lighting a lamp to show the way back into the world.

They have gathered on Sunday. On this Lord's day they have gathered and have read, listened, prayed, preached, and eaten. This is the Lord's Supper.

Remember Who You Are

Whenever today's Christians gather for the Lord's Supper, one of the reasons we gather is to remember. In gathering, let us remember some of the meals in our past: covenant, Passover, sacrifice, the Last Supper, Emmaus, Pentecost, and beyond. These are some of the memories of meals which enrich our present mealtimes with the Lord when we "do this in remembrance of" him.

Remembrance. Our remembrance at the Lord's Table in the Lord's Supper is no mere historical recollection. It is not as if we are having a memorial meal for some beloved but departed friend. We are not at a wake for a dead hero. Our friend Jesus is not dead, not departed, not some distant memory. He is presently reigning Lord. So how are we to remember him?

We use that word *remember* in a twofold sense. We say, "Remember George Washington." Thus, we recollect the memory of a famous but dead hero. We remember that at one time there was a man named Washington who lived and achieved but is now dead. This is *historical remembrance.*

But we have another sense in which we use the word *remember.* Sometimes we say, "Remember who you are." I tell my children when I take them to a friend's, "You are expected to behave." We discuss some difficult problem at our church board meeting and someone says, "Remember now, we are the church and we ought to do the Christian thing in this situation." In such cases, *remember* does not mean mere historical recollection. It more nearly means *to wake up, to open your eyes, to call to mind, to renew or reawaken. Remember who you are.*

This second, more dynamic and profound, sense of *remember* is how we are best to remember Christ in the Lord's Supper. When some people come to the Lord's Supper they come with long faces and sad hearts, as if they are at a funeral, as if their best friend has just died, or at least as if their best friend died 2,000 years ago. But our best friend has *not* died! Christ is present, alive, at work in the world, in the midst of us. We do not have to work hard to remember Christ in the sense of a long-departed person. We are to remember him in the sense of, "Wake up, he's here"; or, "Open your eyes, your Lord and friend is with you"; or, "Remember who you are." Against our Monday-through-Saturday amnesia, we gather on Sunday to eat and to remember Jesus' words:

> Where two or three are gathered in my name, there am I in the midst of them.
>
> —Matthew 18:20

And so, when we gather with our brothers and sisters in Christ, when the bread is broken and blessed, when the bread and wine are given, we joyfully remember that he is in the midst of us. Like the earliest disciples at that Sunday evening dinner at Emmaus, our "eyes [are] opened" and we see (Luke 24:31). And even for us, in our time and place, it can be said as it was said of our forebears in the faith, "They beheld God, and ate and drank" (Exod. 24:11b).

CHAPTER TWO

He Took Bread and Blessed It

When he was at table with them, he took the bread
and blessed, and broke it, and gave it to them. And their
eyes were opened and they recognized him.
—Luke 24:30-31a

Signs of Love

Gazing out of my office window on this cold, gray January day, I became conscious that I was moving my wedding ring around my finger. I glanced down at the ring, a simple band of gold which my wife slipped on my finger on a hot June Saturday over eleven years ago. It is just a piece of metal. To the outside observer it is worth little more than the gold it took to make it. But to me, alone and gazing out my window on this lonely, cold day, it is a warming, enduring, tangible, visible symbol of the love which someone has for me. That is priceless.

To an outside, detached observer, the bread and wine which we share at the Lord's Supper is just that—bread and wine. But to the disciple, these humble, ordinary things are enduring, tangible, visible symbols of God's love. To the detached, outside observer, the man Jesus looks like a typical, young carpenter of first-century Judea. But to the disciple, this man is the visible symbol of God's love. "Don't tell me, show me," we say. Frequently we want more than words. Actions speak louder than words.

God knows this. In the Bible, God not only says, "I love you," through the words of the law, the prophets, the sermons of Jesus, the letters of Paul. God's love is also demonstrated through signs and sign-acts. "And this will be a sign for you: you will find a babe wrapped in swaddling clothes and lying in a manger" (Luke 2:12). The babe at Bethlehem is a sign that God is acting to redeem his people.

Love is demonstrated through symbols. At a wedding, words of love are spoken by a man and woman—big, important words like *love, cherish, honor,* and *keep.* But rings are also given with the explanation, "The wedding ring is the outward and visible sign of an inward and spiritual grace." The rings are symbols of the covenant this man and woman have made—visible, tangible ways of showing some of the deepest and most inexpressible feelings in their lives.

A flag, a handshake, a kiss, a cross, a wedding ring, a loaf of bread, a chalice of wine—all are symbols which say more than words can express. A symbol opens up a level of reality for which non-symbolic speaking is inadequate. There is no other way to *say* what a symbol expresses except to refer to the symbol. Try to explain a beautiful painting you have just seen to someone who has never seen it. Try to make someone else feel what you felt when you saw a movie last night without his or her having seen it. It is difficult.

Unfortunately, in our abstracted, verbal, word-oriented culture, we often overlook the power of the symbolic. Sometimes Protestants say, "The bread and wine of Holy Communion is *only a symbol* of Christ." *Only* a symbol? Talk of this kind implies that there is something more than the symbolic—namely, the verbal or the literal. But the point I am trying to make is the literal and the verbal are not *more* than the symbolic, but less. It would be more accurate to say that something was *only a word,* for words are often intangible, abstract, vague, and generalized. Words themselves are symbols—somewhat abstracted, intangible symbols.

That lump in your throat when you see our country's flag go by in a parade, that horrible sense of loss you felt when you lost your wedding ring, the cross which stands atop your church's steeple, or, for that matter, a Nazi swastika or a Ku Klux Klan burning cross—can you honestly say these are merely symbols?

It is part of the nature of symbols that they are transparent to that which they symbolize. They evoke that reality, open it up to us, make it accessible to our senses.

Jesus himself is the supreme, visible, tangible symbol which expresses and reveals God's love for humanity.

And the Word became flesh and dwelt among us, full of grace and truth; we have beheld his glory, glory as of the only Son from the Father. . . . And from his fullness have we all received, grace upon grace. . . . No one has ever seen God; the only Son, who is in the bosom of the Father, he has made him known.

—John 1:14-18

Sacraments

Most powerful and evocative of all the symbolic demonstrations of God's love is God's gift of the *sacraments*. Sacraments are signs in that they are actions, like feeding and washing, which are full of deep meaning. They are symbols in that they are objects like bread, wine, and water which are packed with significance.

Sometimes we get confused into thinking that Christianity is a *spiritual* religion, as if our faith is mostly a matter of ethereal, intangible, otherworldly things. Nothing could be further from the faith as Jesus preached it.

Jesus had a way of taking the stuff of everyday life—coins, mustard seeds, daily work, water, bread, wine—and using them to help us see the presence of God in our midst. Jesus himself was the Incarnation, God "in the flesh." By his very presence, Jesus witnessed to a God who, in God's great love, chose to use earthly, physical objects and actions to reveal himself to us. John Calvin once said, in effect, that God never forgets that we are creatures and so uses creaturely things through which to love us. Elsewhwere, in speaking of the mystery of the Lord's Supper, Calvin says, "God imports spiritual things under visible ones."

One of the main differences between Christianity and the world's other great religions is its use of material things in its worship. Archbishop William Temple said that the best evidence for claiming that Christianity is the true faith "lies in the fact that it is the most avowedly materialistic of all the great religions."[1] The difference between Christianity and religions which have no incarnation is the difference between receiving a letter from someone you love and having the loved one embrace you. A letter is fine, as far as words go, but nothing beats a hug from your beloved! Every time we look at Jesus we are reminded: Our God did not simply write a letter or send a sermon; our God got into the act of the drama of salvation. Our God did not abandon the world or urge us to abandon it. Our God's love was not content to remain aloof, off in the clouds somewhere; that love came in the flesh, in a manger, in a young Jew from Nazareth, on a cross. It is this visible, tangible, fleshly, material nature of God's love which St. Augustine had in mind when he called Christ "the sacrament of God."

Some people look for a religion which is invisible, angelic, spiritual, and ethereal, untouched by human hands and mother earth. There may be such a religion, but Christianity is not it. We cannot separate body from soul, sex from love, job from vocation, earth from heaven, or money from religion. "God likes matter; he invented it," said C. S. Lewis.

> For surely it is not with angels that [Christ] is concerned but with the descendants of Abraham. Therefore he had to be made like his brethren in every respect.
>
> —Hebrews 2:16-17a

"Not with angels is our God concerned!" says the writer of Hebrews. Thank God! For we are not angels. We are men and women, flesh and blood. We live here, on earth, not in some spiritual Shangri-la in the clouds. We live here, with junior's spilled cereal and with a cancer that will not heal and pain that will not go away and with gnawing hunger and parched lips. This is where we live. And this is where, as the Bible tells Jesus' story, God meets us.

We are forever getting confused into thinking that God wants to meet us somewhere else, in some holy land. Not here, in Greenville, South Carolina or Sydney, Australia, or Fargo, North Dakota. Not here at my morning breakfast table. Not at my church. We are forever thinking that it is in some mountaintop experience, in some moment of spiritual ecstasy, some emotional high, some religious trip that God meets us. So we search for the Holy Land, we venerate the relics, we try to tune in or tune out, escape, or whatever. All this is part of our fantasy that God is somewhere other than here, among some other people than us.

But where did Jesus himself say he would meet us? Broken body and shed blood, ordinary bread and everyday wine, common people and your usual friends. He meets you here.

As Elizabeth Barrett Browning wrote in "Aurora Leigh":

> Earth's crammed with heaven,
> And every common bush afire with God;
> But only he who sees takes off his shoes;
> The rest sit round it and pluck blackberries.

Sacraments are our "outward and visible signs of an inward and spiritual grace." But that still sounds a bit mystical, a bit ethereal and distant. A better definition might be: *Sacraments are visible and physical acts of God's self-giving love.*

We have seen God's self-giving love in Christ when "the Word became flesh and dwelt among us" (John 1:14a). In Christ, God's love was made visible. God knows that we can give nothing to him, so God gives to us. God knows that we have failed to find him, so God finds us. God knows that we cannot, on our own, return to him; so God turns to us. He says, "Have some bread. Take some wine. This is my body and my blood, your nourishment and your life." Self-giving love. Communion is as much something which God does as something we do. It is a gift of love.

You have been walking all day. You have no money. You have not eaten for two days now. Your stomach is empty; gnawing hunger consumes your every thought. You feel weak; your head is starting to feel dizzy. A friend sees you. The friend invites you in and puts a plate of warm, hearty soup and a loaf of fresh, home-baked bread before you and bids you eat. You do not have to be told, "This meal is an act of self-giving love." You know.

You have tried to find God. But every way you have taken has turned into a blind alley. Time and again you were sure you had found the way, the life, the truth, only to be disappointed, frustrated, deceived. And you have tried to be good, to do right. But the good you would do, you have not done. Even your best-intentioned efforts have turned out wrong. You have yielded to temptation in spite of your efforts to resist. Everywhere you turn, you are convinced that you are no good, worthless, without hope. A friend comes to you. That friend finds you where you are. He accepts you, welcomes you, embraces you. He reassures you and urges you to go on. Finally, he takes your punishment, pays your debt, dies in your behalf. You do not have to be told, "This is friendship, this is an act of self-giving love." You know.

Israel had always seen food as a gift of God. Thus the Jews always gave thanks before meals. Israel's God is the God who gave quail in the wilderness (Exod. 16) and water from the rock (Exod. 17) so that the chosen people might not perish. The ravens bring Elijah food so that God's fearless prophet was saved (1 Kings 17:6). Here is a God who "satisfies him who is thirsty, and the hungry he fills with good things" (Psalm 107:9). In a land of abundant food, we tend to forget that food itself is one of the most basic, most continual, most ever-present signs of God's self-giving love. "O taste and see that the Lord is good!" says the psalmist (34:8).

> The eyes of all look to thee,
> and thou givest them their food in due season.
> Thou openest thy hand,
> thou satisfiest the desire of every living thing.
> —Psalm 145:15-16

How typical of Jesus, when he came to the end of his earthly ministry, to take one of the most simple and ordinary of human experiences —sharing food together in a common meal—and celebrate it as a symbol of his whole life and work. Not only that meal in the upper room, but also every meal which Jesus ate with his disciples, was a sign of Jesus' presence here among us. At all of these meals when "he was at table with them," Jesus was doing with his disciples what he did with them throughout his ministry, in his stories and sermons, his healings, his death on the cross, his resurrection, and his gift of Spirit—*giving himself to them in order that they might experience the near love of God and be empowered to do God's will.*

"Don't tell me; show me," humanity says to its Creator down through the ages. And so God gives us the Christ:

> In many and various ways God spoke of old to our fathers by the prophets; but in these last days he has spoken to us by a Son.
> —Hebrews 1:1-2

And then the Christ gives us himself:

> The Lord Jesus on the night when he was betrayed took bread, and when he had given thanks, he broke it, and said, "This is my body which is broken for you. Do this in remembrance of me." In the same way also the cup, after supper, saying, "This cup is the new covenant in my blood. Do this, as often as you drink it, in remembrance of me."
> —1 Corinthians 11:23b-25

The Real Presence

In the beginning, the church simply affirmed that the risen Christ was present in its midst, on the basis of Christ's promise, "Lo, I am with you always" (Matt. 28:20), and on the basis of its own experience. Later, particularly in the Middle Ages, laborious attempts were made to explain how and when Christ was present in the Lord's Supper. Complicated philosophical theories such as transubstantiation were devised to explain the nature of Christ's presence at the meal. (*Transubstantiation* is the belief that the substance of the bread and wine is transformed into the substance of the flesh and blood of Christ, even though the outward appearance of the bread and wine remain unchanged.)

The medieval church came to believe that at the moment the priest repeated the words, "This is my body," over the bread on the altar, a mysterious and miraculous change took place in which the bread was transformed into the physical presence of Christ.

While these theories of the real presence of Christ in the meal may have helped people and while they were originally designed to correct superstitious abuses of the sacrament, their ultimate effect was to split the church by arguments over the nature, mode, moment, and conditions for the real presence of Christ in the Supper.

Protestant Reformers, while affirming Christ's presence at the church's celebrations of the sacrament, were disturbed because many of the faithful avoided the Lord's Supper (or the *Mass,* as it was called during the Middle Ages) out of fear of somehow profaning or desecrating the body and blood of their Lord. The reformers sought to recover a more dynamic sense of the presence.

Fortunately, Protestants and Roman Catholics have moved beyond these old debates to a more fruitful and common recognition of Christ's presence. All affirm that while the manner and means of the self-giving love of Christ's presence within the meal may remain mysteries to us, we are nevertheless sure of his real presence with us.

Unfortunately, some Protestants assume that if they do not believe in the docrine of transubstantiation, they do not believe in the real presence of Christ in his Supper. The Supper thus becomes little more than a memorial commemorating Christ's real absence rather than his real presence! Nothing could be more contrary to the witness of scripture and to our tradition. We may not believe that Christ is *on* this table in the sense that a miraculous physical change has occurred in the composition of the bread and wine. We may not be able to specify the *when* or the *how* of this presence. But we certainly believe that Christ is present *at* this table *with* his gathered people.

This is not so much something to be proven as it is something to be experienced. John Calvin spoke for us all when he said of the mystery of Christ's presence in the Lord's Supper, "I would rather experience it than understand it." And I imagine that you have already experienced that presence. How often have you come to worship, unwilling, expecting nothing, unseeking, only to be caught off guard by the near presence of

God? Like John Wesley the night he went unwillingly to a little meeting on London's Aldersgate Street, we are sometimes surprised by God, surprised by God's presence. We come expecting to be the only one at the meeting, only to find that God is already there, waiting for us, expecting us, even pursuing us.

I say this because in my own life this presence has so often been unwelcome. I can think of as many reasons for wanting to avoid God as for wanting to meet him. But there God is. We sit down for a little meal, a little polite religious conversation, and a little folksy Sunday fellowship. Then, before you know it, we are moved to tears, we stand naked before the truth, a voice penetrates the meaningless chatter, there is a rushing wind through our desert, and we know we are not alone.

Protestants do believe in the real presence of Christ at the Lord's Supper. In the bread and the wine, in the table talk and fellowship, Protestants believe they are brought very close to the Lord. As one of Charles Wesley's communion hymns puts it:

> O the depth of love divine, Th' unfathomable
>   grace!
> Who shall say how bread and wine God into
>   man conveys!
> How the bread his flesh imparts, How the wine
>   transmits his blood,
> Fills his faithful people's hearts With all the life
>   of God!
> Sure and real is the grace, The manner be
>   unknown;
> Only meet us in thy ways And perfect us in one.
> Let us taste the heavenly powers; Lord, we ask
>   for nothing more.
> Thine to bless, 'tis only ours To wonder and
>   adore. Amen.

I think the church erred when it tried to define Christ's presence in terms of time and place. How can we say that Christ is more present in the repetition of the words, "This is my body," than he is present in the breaking of the loaf? How can we say that he is more present in the loaf than he is present in those who break and share the bread and bless and pass the cup? Christ is present here and now, in terms of time and space, but most importantly, he is present to us as a person, a friend.

The real presence is a *personal presence*.[2] When my friend is with me, it means more to me than that he is here in this place and at this mo-

Cornelius O'Sullivan Chalice
Ireland, 1597

ment. He is here *for me*. He is here as one who loves and is loved. Sometimes my friend is with me in a manner which transcends time and space. For instance, when my friend calls me on the telephone, he becomes really present for me, though he is not spatially present. When I, rummaging through a cluttered drawer, come across an old photograph of me and my friend on a winter camping trip long ago, suddenly my friend is present personally, even though he is not present either at this time or in this place. Personal presence implies communion, a meeting of persons that is deep and moving, that goes beyond time and place.

These experiences of presence in everyday life should warn us against trying to fix too precisely the place or the moment of Christ's presence in the Lord's Supper. This does not mean that when we speak of Christ being present, we are talking about a presence which is only "spiritual" or diffuse. When I sit in the presence of someone I love, I am not sitting in the presence of love in the abstract; I am sitting in his or her concrete, physical presence. There is no way for me to love my friend without loving my friend as a person with definite characteristics, as an embodied presence. My friend's presence is *real;* it is not simply a noble thought about friendship in general.

Certainly Christ is always and everywhere present in the world. But he is particularly, intimately present to us in Holy Communion. If he were simply contained in every rock, tree, and glade, as a pantheist might claim, then it would make no sense to talk about his presence anywhere. Christ would be too diffuse and abstract. One does not speak of the presence of oxygen. It is always there, floating about, so its presence is of no particular note.

While we believe that God is universally present at all times and places, it is important not to let our experiences of God's particular presence get swallowed up in that universal presence. We are not related to an abstract, generalized notion of the divine in general. We are in love with the God of Abraham, Isaac, and Jacob. We are in the particular presence of Jesus of Nazareth. We are being met by the Holy Spirit, not just spirit in general.

We would never experience the universal presence of Christ if we were not pointed to it by a multitude of particular presences—those moments and places in life when Christ seems particularly close to us with an undeniable intensity. It is part of our human need to seek some ark, some tabernacle, some holy of holies, some focal point of meeting where God is experienced with definiteness and particular intensity. Once again, when I am in the presence of my friend, whether it is his presence in the form of a visit, a letter, or that moment of recognition when I pick up the tennis racket which he gave me, I am in the presence of a particular friend who has a particular name, a particular face, a particular personality. There can be no person without embodiment. And so we are pointed to things, things like the Bible and bread and wine and water and the church, and we are invited to experience these as indications, illuminations, catalysts of Christ's presence. This is the way we can speak of Christ as present in the Lord's Supper.

The Second Vatican Council said it this way:

> Christ is always present in His Church, especially in her liturgical celebrations. He is present in the sacrifice of the Mass, not only in the person of His minister, . . . but especially under the Eucharistic species. By His power He is present in the sacraments, so that when a man baptizes it is really Christ Himself who baptizes. He is present in His word, since it is He Himself who speaks when the holy Scriptures are read in the church. He is present, finally, when the Church prays and sings, for He promised: "Where two or three are gathered together for my sake, there am I in the midst of them" (Matt. 18:20).
>
> Christ indeed always associates the Church with Himself in the truly great work of giving perfect praise to God and making men holy.[3]

Leo the Great once said of the bread of the Lord's Supper that it "makes conspicuous" Christ's presence among us. Without that bread and wine, without that gathered congregation and its prayers, without that sermon and the eating and drinking, we might be blind to that presence. But because these gifts of love are present for us, Christ is present also. How? I do not know how. I only know it is so. Such close love is always a mystery. As Charles Wesley wrote,

> Sure and real is the grace,
> The manner be unknown; . . .
> Thine to bless, 'tis only ours
> To wonder and adore.

The Self-Giving of God

On the night in which he was betrayed and given up to death, Jesus took bread and, as he had done so often, blessed it, broke it, and gave it to his disciples. He blessed it. Bread, one of the most basic of all God's gifts and human creations, was blessed. Before the bread, there had been seed, the thousands of seeds scattered across some hillside. The fields had been plowed. The rains watered. The soil had been fertilized and tilled and nurtured until the wheat was brought to full growth. Then it was harvested, gathered, and ground into flour. The flour was mixed with shortening, salt, yeast, and milk. It became batter, then dough; then the dough was kneaded and shaped into loaves where it was allowed to rise. Then it was baked.

All of this—the soil, the farmer, the sower, the miller, the baker, the earthly, the corporeal, the commercial, the creaturely, the mundane stuff of everyday life—all of this was blessed. All of this was claimed by Christ as part of the self-giving love of God. All of this became sacramental.

Never again, after that blessing, can we look upon a field of grain or a loaf of Communion bread or a slice of breakfast toast in the same casual way we did before. God is in all that, in the people who work with them, in the people who partake of them, in us. That bread might end up on the Lord's table, being blessed as part of the Lord's Supper. Even if it does not, Jesus has blessed it. "This is my body . . . for you," he has said (1 Cor. 11:24). For you.

He took bread and blessed it. And thereby we are blessed.

CHAPTER THREE

Let the Party Begin

This, the first of his signs, Jesus did at Cana in Galilee, and manifested his glory; and his disciples believed in him.

—John 2:11

Water to Wine

One of the Pharisees' chief criticisms of Jesus was not that his theology was bad but that Jesus was "a man gluttonous, and a winebibber" (Matt. 11:18-19, KJV).

John chooses to begin his gospel at, of all places, a wedding party, with Jesus doing, of all things, a transformation of water into wine. I can think of a thousand more appropriate ways to begin a ministry. Why not a healing (the way Mark begins) or an inaugural sermon (the way Luke begins) or at least the production of something more nourishing? At least some act more edifying than the quick fermentation of twenty or thirty gallons to keep a party from pooping? Is this any way for a Savior to practice salvation?

What a frivolous, useless, pointless miracle that was.

The spirit of the wedding party starts to lag; the wine is almost gone; the revelers come to Jesus. At his instructions, water is turned to wine. This act is said to have "manifested his glory" (John 2:11). But where is the glory in that? I, son of the Puritans that I am, want to know.

The Gift of Food

In the beginning, in Genesis, humanity is given food by God (see Gen. 1:30, 2:16).

> All look to thee,
>   to give them their food in due season.
> When thou givest to them, they gather it up;
>   when thou openest thy hand, they are filled with good things.
> —Psalm 104:27-28

Ecclesiastes rejoices that "bread is made for laughter, and wine gladdens life" (Eccles. 10:19). This divine gift not only sustains life but also makes living a joy:

> There is nothing better for a man than that he should eat and drink, and find enjoyment in his toil. This also, I saw, is from the hand of God; for apart from him who can eat or who can have enjoyment?
> —Ecclesiastes 2:24-25

Food is a gift rather than a right, "God's gift to man" (Eccles. 3:13), received "from the hand of God."

The Gospels depict Jesus as a giver of food and drink. The wedding at Cana, the miraculous catch of fish (Luke 5:1-11), the feeding of the multitude (recorded in all the Gospels, compare Luke 9:10-17), and the meals of John 21 are all significant, miraculous occasions where Jesus provides the meal. In succeeding chapters in this book we will focus upon some of these meals with Jesus.

Of course, like any other of God's gifts, the gift of food can be abused. In a nation where two chief health problems are obesity and alcoholism, do we need to be reminded of the potentially destructive, dangerous, demonic aspects of these gifts?

Like the gift of sex, the gifts of food and drink can be used irresponsibly, can destroy as easily as they edify. Just as nitroglycerin can both blow up bridges and ease strained hearts, food and drink can be destructive as well as constructive. The Bible knows this two-sided coin. The psalmist praises God for the gift of wine "to gladden the heart of man" (Psalm 104:15), but the prophet warns that "wine is treacherous" (Hab. 2:5). Proverbs says that even this divine gift is a "mocker" and a "brawler" (20:1). Old Noah disembarks from the ark to become the "first tiller of the soil" (Gen. 9:20), the first human to exercise the divinely given creativity and productivity in agriculture. But farmer Noah is also the first to plant a vineyard, get drunk, go naked, and make a fool of himself (Gen. 9:20-25).

If you have never known what it is to toss and turn all night, mumbling through your indigestion, "I can't believe I ate the whole thing," then I suppose you do not understand what happened to Noah. But if you have felt the satiated excesses of gluttony or felt your head swimming and reeling with alcohol-induced stupor, then you know firsthand the reality of this two-fold nature of food and drink.

Jesus commanded his followers to "do this in remembrance of me," and yet gluttony and drunkenness appear to have blotched the early church's sacred meals (1 Cor. 11:21; Jude, v. 12; 2 Pet. 2:13). Paul says that there are those in the church who "do not serve our Lord Christ, but their own appetites" (Rom. 16:18) and whose "god is the belly" (Phil. 3:19).

Little wonder, then, that some should try to overcome this treacherous dualism of food and drink with asceticism and self-denial. Perhaps the sin of abusing food and drink could be avoided by abstaining from food and drink, they reasoned. Fasting thus became a hot issue for the early church.

In the Old Testament, fasting is a sign of repentance. If feasting is a sign of festivity and joy, fasting is a sign of grief and mourning. When Saul dies, the nation fasts (1 Sam. 31:13). Fasting was often accompanied by the wearing of sackcloth and ashes. On the day of atonement, when Israel confessed her sin, the nation fasted.

The prophets sometimes condemned fasting when it became a substitute for works of righteousness. Then, as now, people sometimes used their religion and religious acts such as fasting as a way to avoid practicing their religion in works of love.

> Will you call this a fast,
>   and a day acceptable to the Lord?
> Is not this the fast that I choose:
>   to loose the bonds of wickedness,
>   to undo the thongs of the yoke,
> to let the oppressed go free,
>   and to break every yoke?
> Is it not to share your bread with
>   the hungry,
> and bring the homeless poor into
>   your house?
>   —Isaiah 58:5b-7a

Jesus fasts when he goes into the wilderness (Matt. 4:1f.), probably reflecting the Jewish custom of individual fasting during times of personal supplication of preparation to receive divine vision. After he eats the Passover (Luke 22:16), Jesus fasts before his death.

Some early Christians did not eat flesh or drink wine (Rom. 14:1f.). These were probably the same ascetics who did not marry (1 Cor. 7:25f.) and who held no possessions (Matt. 10:9f.; Acts 2:44f.). Paul is troubled by these practices and their effect upon the Body of Christ (the church).

The presence of those who fasted in the church led to conflicts between what Paul calls the "strong" and the "weak." Note who Paul calls the "strong"—those who are free to eat and to drink all things with thankfulness. The "weak" are vegetarians and total abstainers. The "strong" and the "weak" came into conflict. In the church at Rome, there were "disputes over opinions" (Rom. 14:1) where the opposing factions despised and passed judgment on one another (Rom. 14:3, 4, 10, 13). They were accused by Paul of putting "a stumbling-block or hindrance in the way of a brother" (Rom. 14:13). They even refused to "welcome" one another at the Lord's table. (Rom. 14:1, 15:7).

Why did those whom Paul characterized as "weak in faith" believe that they must be vegetarians and total abstainers? Paul presupposes that they abstained "in honor of the Lord" and in gratitude to God (Rom. 14:6). There is no suggestion that they did what they did to earn spiritual brownie points. They probably abstained for reasons of purity, in order to be free from anxiety about worldly affairs, in order to be sure that they kept clean from polluting contact with pagan practices and foods. What we have here is possibly an overly scrupulous, cautious asceticism which separates the world into the clean and the unclean as far as food is concerned.

This attitude is attacked:

> Now the Spirit expressly says that in later times some will depart from the faith by giving heed to deceitful spirits and doctrines . . . , who forbid marriage and enjoin abstinence from foods which God created to be received with thanksgiving by those who believe and know the truth. For everything created by God is good, and nothing is to be rejected if it is received with thanksgiving.
>
> —I Timothy 4:1, 3-4

The gnostics, who believed that the world was dualistically divided into flesh and spirit, evil and good, darkness and light, protested strongly against certain foods which they thought to be unclean.

Peter himself struggled with foods which his Jewish heritage had taught him to regard as "unclean" (Acts 10-11). Peter was in Joppa. About noon he went up to the top floor of a friend's house to pray. While praying, he became hungry, so hungry that he fell into a trance and had a vision. In the vision, all kinds of animals appeared on a sheet being let down from heaven. "Rise, Peter; kill and eat," a voice said.

Peter, good orthodox Jew that he was, refused. "No, Lord; for I have never eaten anything that is common or unclean."

"Don't call God's creations common or unclean," said the voice.

Peter wondered what all this meant. He soon found out. Cornelius, an Italian army officer, sent for Peter and invited him to eat dinner with him. While there at the table, Cornelius got to hear about Jesus. Cornelius, Gentile that he was, asked to be baptized. Peter consented, saying, "Truly I perceive that God shows no partiality" (Acts 10:34).

When Peter got back to Jerusalem, he was accosted by the circumcision party. "Why did you go to these Gentiles and eat with them?" they wanted to know. How dare you eat unclean foods with the unclean? How dare you fail to make proper distinction? (Acts 11:3, author's paraphrase).

"The Spirit told me to go with them without hesitation" (Acts 11:12), was Peter's defense of his unorthodox eating habits.

Against a dualistic attitude toward food, the writer of First Timothy stresses food as a gift of God to be received, like all God's gifts, with thanksgiving. "Thus he declared all foods clean" (Mark 7:19). As Peter discovered, words like *clean* and *unclean* are removed from the Christian's culinary vocabulary by Christ's redeeming work. The "strong" are those who see that all of God's gifts are good and all are to be received and enjoyed with thanksgiving. Through the ages, ascetic and monastic movements which sought to purify themselves from contact with the world have often been rightly accused of escapism, quietism, otherworldliness, legalism, and works-righteousness.

Concerning food, Paul seems to say, the essential thing is to receive it with thanksgiving. Our blessings, our prayers of thanksgiving at the table, claim our meat and drink as gifts of God, set our eating and drinking in a sacred context, and transform our eating and drinking into worship. Thus at the Lord's Supper the priest has traditionally held the bread and the cup before the people with these words of invitation: *The Gifts of God for the People of God.*

Paul says that Christians are free to eat all gifts given by God: fish and fowl, meat offered to idols, snails, chocolate sodas with whipped cream, spaghetti, pork—with one major limitation. Because of the "weak" (those who are overly concerned about what they eat and drink), the "strong" may need to abstain in order that our delightful freedom in food not be a cause for our brother or sister's falling (1 Cor. 8:13). *Love* is the only limitation placed upon our eating and drinking.

> "All things are lawful," but not all things build up. Let no one seek his own good, but the good of his neighbor. Eat whatever is sold in the meat market without raising any question on the ground of conscience. For "the earth is the Lord's, and everything in it." . . . Whether you eat or drink, or whatever you do, do all to the glory of God.
>
> —1 Corinthians 10:23b-26, 31

For the sake of "weaker" brothers and sisters, in our eating and drinking as in any other exercise of our Christian freedom, we may voluntarily abstain from some things in order not to give offense to the weak.

How curiously have we used this talk of "strong" and "weak." When I was growing up, we were often told to abstain from alcohol. One of the reasons frequently given went thus: Of course, you might never become an alcoholic, but because you drink, some weaker person might drink and eventually become an alcoholic.

This is curious since the New Testament talk about the "weak" is clearly applied to the abstainers, not the indulgers!

Once, after a long struggle with a person who was caught in the grip of alcoholism, I asked a leader in the Alcoholics Anonymous group in our town how helpful the Christian faith was in overcoming the problem of alcohol addiction. He replied, "As most churches practice Christianity, it is more hurtful than helpful. Ninety percent of my alcoholic friends begin their life story with, 'I was raised in a good Christian home.' Most Christians use alcohol to draw lines between the sinful and the religious, the good and the bad. And you can guess which side the "good" are on. This attitude produces the guilt, feelings of unworthiness, and defeated spirits which are fertile soil for alcoholism."

The "demon" in the alcohol is not in the product itself but in our abuse of it. The same can be said for the "demon" in our problem of overeating. The problem is in the abuse of one of God's gifts, not in the gift itself. No, more than likely, the "demon" is in our seemingly never-ending penchant to use anything—including food and drink—to build walls between ourselves, to set up barriers between the righteous and the unrighteous so that we can assure ourselves that our slate is clean and that we are on the right side —"I may not be the best person in the world, but at least I'm better than that fat slob."

"Sure, I have my problems, but she is nothing but a drunk."

Who are the "strong" and who are the "weak"?

We find that the abuse of food and drink is not so much a matter of *what* we eat and *what* we drink but *how* we eat and drink. When we eat and drink in an unthankful, unredeemed manner, our eating and drinking become a source of pride and division, smugness and separation. This is less than for "the glory of God."

Some in the church sought to avoid problems caused by eating and drinking by avoiding certain foods and drink altogether. By fasting, they reasoned, they could avoid the temptation occasioned by certain foods.

The Pharisees and the disciples of John the Baptist fasted. But the disciples of Jesus ate and drank. Their behavior caused problems for Jesus early in his ministry. When questioned about why his disciples were able to eat, drink, and be merry, Jesus replied in effect, "When the bridegroom finally arrives, the wine is poured and the music is turned up and the party begins" (Matt. 9:14-15, author's paraphrase).

Fasting was a sign of sin, sickness, and death. It was the display of godly sorrow, mourning, and repentence. No doubt, for many practitioners of fasting, it also displayed that they were somehow superior in their righteousness when compared to all those lax "gluttons and winebibbers," as they called Jesus and his disciples. Eating and drinking, on the other hand, were and are signs of reconciliation and peace, of resurrection and life, of thanksgiving and joy, of festivity and hope. Although only one meal is said to have been a "breakfast," all eating and drinking with Jesus was, in a profound sense, a breaking of the fast.

At the Passover, in Luke's Gospel, Jesus said he would not eat or drink again until his kingdom had come. Later, in his meal at Emmaus, at the breakfast on the beach and others, his post-resurrection eating and drinking became a visible sign of the inbreaking kingdom. The fast has been broken. The kingdom is come. Let the party begin!

In the kingdom, God's gifts may be misused. Life in the midst of the kingdom does not protect us from abuse of any of God's gifts, as the squabbles of the early church show. So we must use God's gifts with care, sensitivity to the needs and limitations of others, and love for all—especially those who, because of our selfishness and abuse, suffer a lack of God's gift of food.

Some of my friends have voluntarily decided to be vegetarians out of a deep concern for the world hunger problem. The way they see it, if they abstain from meat, they indirectly provide more grain for the world's hungry. The same argument could be made for abstaining from alcohol in order to preserve more grain for bread. Of course, my personal abstinence from meat or alcohol alone will not insure more bread on some hungry brother or sister's table, but it will help me keep that brother or sister's hunger before me in a visible, continual way—as well as to witness to others.

But Paul's struggle with the abstainers in Corinth and Rome should warn us about the dangers of being self-righteous and overly scrupulous with regard to our eating and drinking. When our eating and drinking put up barriers between us and our brothers and sisters in Christ, it is not something in which to take pride, but rather a curse.

To eat is to admit to the reality of one's hunger, to yoke oneself to other human beings in their hungers, to acknowledge oneself as dependent upon God and others for the necessities of life. To say, "Thanks," is to admit the presence of a gift. To recognize something as a gift is to admit our need. When we eat, we acknowledge our share in the need to be fed and in so doing display our most basic humanity in common with others. Eating and drinking yoke us in solidarity with our brothers and sisters in Christ. And so we come very close to the mystery of the Lord's Supper.

The Glory amidst the Ordinary

Jesus said that his teachings were like newly-fermented wine, so new and effervescent that this good news cannot be contained in the old wineskins of the old-time religion. Perhaps John had something like this in mind when he told the story of Jesus at the wedding in Cana. The earthenware jars held water for the "rites of purification" (John 2:6). This was ceremonial water which was used in certain purifying rites. In changing the water into wine, perhaps John saw the transformation of the old ritualism into a new, spirit-filled vision. It is significant that Jesus begins his ministry in John, not with a sermon, a lecture, or even some good work of healing, exorcism, or enlightenment. He begins at a place as raucous and joyful as a wedding, with something so shocking and frivolous as turning water into wine to pick up a sagging party.

Once again, this Messiah bursts the boundaries of our puny notions of God, religion, right and wrong, good and bad. Unlike the disciples of the austere John the Baptist with their long faces and sad looks, Jesus comes eating and drinking and partying. He agrees that "bread is made for laughter, and wine gladdens life" (Eccles. 10:19).

While not denying the demonic and twofold nature of our eating and drinking, while not overlooking our tendency to use even the best of God's gifts for our own selfish ends, Jesus invites us to eat, drink, and be merry. While not denying the sadness, the pain, the hurt of the world, he gathers up all that and puts it in a new perspective. He throws a party, inviting those who suffer and hurt and hunger. He thus fulfills the prophets' hope that Israel would see a day when the "vats shall overflow with wine" (Joel 2:24), when all of God's hungry ones will be filled with good things. That day is now.

To all those who cry with the psalmist, "My soul thirsts for God, for the living God" (Psalm 42:2*a*), Jesus gives an invitation to his feast of life with the thundering words,

> I am the bread of life; he who comes to me shall not hunger, and he who believes in me shall never thirst.
> —John 6:35

This gracious invitation puts all our eating and drinking in proper perspective. No longer need we satiate ourselves in selfish gluttony, stuffing our faces in a vain attempt to fill our empty hearts. No longer need we drink ourselves into dizzy stupors in attempts to take away the pain, to relieve the hurt, to make ourselves forget. We are loved. Our God has come to us. Our God prepares a table for us in the midst of our enemies and invites us to the head table at the feast.

The Savior drank the vinegar of human cruelty to the dregs; he thirsted; he hungered; he tasted the bitterness of it all before, with us. In so doing he became a sign of God for us, *pro nobis, pro mundo* (for us, for the world). *He turned the water into wine.* In so doing he showed us a sign, a manifestation of his glory. This is the glory of God. For some, the glory of God is manifested in the transcendence or otherness of God—God the remote and the aloof. But John's Gospel speaks of a different glory—a glory whose gloriousness is precisely in its nearness. Here at a wedding party, amid daily cares—cares about what to eat and what to drink, how to control drinking, what to do about weight, how people look at each other—is God in the flesh. This is God with us. *Emmanuel.* This is God understood as a dynamism, an energy, a quality of being, an opening into and expansion of and enrichment in everyday life. "I came that they may have life, and have it abundantly," he says of his glory (John 10:10*b*).

"The Son gives life to whom he will" (John 5:21*b*). The Latin word for banquet, *convivium*, says it better than our English equivalent. To eat and drink in the name of and in the presence of Jesus is to eat "with life" — *convivium*—to share life, to participate in the joy and the festivity which is meant to be at the heart of it all.

After a glimpse of this glory at the wedding at Cana or in the upper room or on the way to Emmaus or before the Lord's table in your own church, you will never again eat and drink the same way. To eat and drink with the Lord at his table illuminates all your meals. Your morning breakfast is no longer the eggs and bacon and soggy cornflakes of the humdrum and the routine; it is transformed into a banquet to be eaten with glad and generous hearts. The morning coffee break, the noonday snack on the assembly line, the sandwich between mowing the hayfields, the evening meal around the family dinner table—all can be done to the glory of God, in response to this glory which is revealed to us in our eating and drinking. All eating can be eucharistic—in joy and thanks. "They said to him, 'Lord, give us this bread *always*' " (John 6:34).

Have patience with me, friend Jesus, as I shuffle around my eggs and bacon on my breakfast plate, as I thoughtlessly gobble down my hamburger at lunch today, as I sullenly eat my supper tonight and correct the children for their bad manners and complain about the high cost of groceries, as I shuffle forward at communion to receive the body and the blood. Forgive me. I know not what I do. I better suit the culinary habits and scornful preaching of John the Baptist than the joyful, playful eating and drinking in your kingdom.

Have patience. I keep getting confused into thinking that discipleship is basically a serious and distasteful affair. I work hard, try to do right, labor to keep my slate clean, follow the rules, watch my habits, watch my friends, and keep myself buttoned down, under control, neat, respectable, serious, and suitably reverent. I come up for communion with an appropriately sad face. I try to have good manners.

Then, just when I figure out which fork to use and have my napkin tucked in neatly and am able to keep the peas on my fork and can drink without the tea dribbling down my chin, then you come along. You, with your pointless frivolity, making fun of my pretend religion, urging me to loosen up. You come along, changing insipid water into rich, bloodred wine; turning this funeral into a banquet; convincing me once again that life is better than death, that the spirit should be let loose, that joy is the serious business of heaven. I see once again that a sad and somber Holy Communion is an affront to the presence of the risen Christ. There is a lot of new wine here, bursting the old wineskins of tired, respectable religion.

I see your glory.

CHAPTER FOUR

What's a Savior Like You Doing with Sinners Like Us?

The Pharisees and their scribes murmured against his disciples, saying, "Why do you eat and drink with tax collectors and sinners?" And Jesus answered them, "Those who are well have no need of a physician, but those who are sick; I have not come to call the righteous, but sinners to repentance."

—Luke 5:30-32

Saints and Sinners

One of the things which angered Jesus' critics was his choice of dinner companions. The way Luke tells it, his friends were a motley crew: tax collectors, Pharisees, harlots, common fishermen, assorted women. The Pharisees kept telling Jesus, "You've got to be careful whom you eat with."

You've got to be careful.

The dinner table is such an intimate, holy, transforming, mysterious place—you've got to be careful whom you eat with.

If you are trying to convince yourself that another person is not a full, valuable, human being, a brother or sister, be careful not to invite that person to dinner. Be careful. Remember, as Oscar Wilde said, "After a good dinner, one could forgive anybody, even one's relatives."

At the House of Levi

Luke says that one of the first people Jesus invited to join the Gospel movement was Levi, a tax collector.

> He went out, and saw a tax collector, named Levi, sitting at the tax office; and he said to him, "Follow me." And he left everything, and rose and followed him.
>
> —Luke 5:27-28

He called a tax collector. Tax collectors are the undisputed bad guys in the Gospels. They were the despised collaborators with the oppressive Roman overlords. They collaborated with the Romans in heaping excessive burdens on people. They delt in filthy lucre stamped with Caesar's image; therefore, they were not only swindlers and traitors—they were idolaters.

This type of person is one of the first whom Jesus called to discipleship and the first, according to Luke, with whom Jesus feasted.

> Levi made him a great feast in his house; and there were a large company of tax collectors and others sitting at table with them.
>
> —Luke 5:29

The Pharisees peered in the doorway and saw Jesus at Levi's table. The sight of Jesus with all these scoundrels was more than the Pharisees could take.

> The Pharisees and their scribes murmured against his disciples, saying, "Why do you eat and drink with tax collectors and sinners?"
>
> —Luke 5:30

The Pharisees admittedly receive a bad press in the Gospels. Luke categorizes the Pharisees as religious snobs, holier-than-thou types who took pride in their adherence to the letter of the law but who had little regard for the needs or limitations of others.

Actually, the Pharisees were a rather liberal party in Judaism. St. Paul was proud of his heritage as a Pharisee. The Pharisees believed in such relatively new ideas as the resurrection of the dead. They sought to apply religion to the dilemmas of everyday life and to practice their faith rigorously.

But Luke depicts the Pharisees as the enemies of Jesus. Jesus calls them hypocrites, whitewashed tombs, implying that they have somehow gotten confused in their zeal, that they are so hung up on minor matters that they "neglect justice and the love of God" (Luke 11:42).

Part of their so-called righteousness demanded that they avoid contact with those whom they regarded as unrighteous. This is what bothers

Ciborium
St. Mark's, Venice — 6th century

them about Jesus' meal with Levi and friends. Jesus replies in effect, "If you are well, you don't need a doctor" (Luke 5:31, author's paraphrase), implying that those who are sickest of all are those who don't know how sick they are. Such was the sickness of the Pharisees.

Jesus tells them, "I have not come to call the righteous, but sinners to repentance" (Luke 5:32). He seeks to call not only Levi but all whom the Pharisees would exclude. *Call* here also means *invite*—as if to invite to a banquet. And that is what he does, saying:

> Blessed are you poor, for yours is the kingdom of God.
> Blessed are you that hunger now, for you shall be satisfied.
> Blessed are you that weep now, for you shall laugh.
>   —Luke 6:20b-21

The Pharisees then want to know why Jesus and his disciples do not fast. They say:

> The disciples of John fast often and offer prayers, and so do the disciples of the Pharisees, but yours eat and drink.
>   —Luke 5:33

In other words, "We can tell that the disciples of John the Baptist are religious; they are always so sad and miserable. But your disciples eat, drink, and make merry. Is that any way for a religious person to act?"

"When a bridegroom shows up at the marriage feast," Jesus replied, "Do the wedding guests feast—or fast? The bridegroom is here, let the party begin" (Luke 5:34, author's paraphrase).

"What is to be done with you?" Jesus wonders aloud to himself. "John came fasting and you said, 'He's a demon.' I come eating and drinking, and you say, 'Behold, a glutton and a drunkard, a friend of tax collectors and sinners!' " (Luke 7:33-34, author's paraphrase).

The time is never quite right; the conditions are never quite suitable; the herald is never quite up to our expectations. And so, we wait.

This new wine (Luke 5:37-39) which bursts the old wineskins is deeply threatening to the petty, moralistic, exclusive piety represented by the Pharisees. Jesus disregarded Sabbath laws by plucking and eating grain (Luke 6:1-5). He shocked the good religious folk by eating with tax collectors and sinners. John the Baptist undoubtedly spoke for many when he asked, "Are you he who is to come, or shall we look for another?" (Luke 7:19). Jesus' answer to John's query reveals the peculiar nature of this kingdom Jesus came to proclaim:

Go and tell John what you have seen and heard: the blind receive
their sight, the lame walk, lepers are cleansed, and the deaf hear, the
dead are raised up, the poor have good news preached to them.
And blessed is he who takes no offense at me.

—Luke 7:22-23

And yet, many were offended. And why not? To have believed
and waited as did so many of God's chosen and to have suffered for that
very chosenness, only to see God's anointed one making no distinction,
breaking the boundaries, inviting the outsiders—who wouldn't take
offense?

After all, what good is my churchgoing, tithing, praying, believing,
and righteousness if God is going to be gracious without making distinction?

Woe to you that are full now, for you shall hunger.

—Luke 6:25

Pharisees and Prostitutes

Having eaten with tax collectors, Jesus now sits at a Pharisee's table
(Luke 7:36f.). There was a woman of the city "who was a sinner" (v. 37).
She heard Jesus was at the Pharisee's home. She went to see Jesus, taking with her a flask of sweet-smelling ointment to anoint him with. And
here's where the trouble began.

She wept, wet Jesus' feet with her tears, let down her hair and
wiped his feet with her hair as she kissed his feet and anointed them with
the ointment.

This was more than the Pharisee could take. "If this man were a real
prophet," the Pharisee muttered to himself, "he would know what sort of
woman this is who touches him, for she is a sinner" (Luke 7:39, author's
paraphrase).

"After all," the Pharisee wanted to know, "What are real prophets
for if not to be able to distinguish between right and wrong, good and bad,
the evil and the just?"

We are not told what her sin was. Some scholars suggest that her
sin might have been prostitution. The flask of sweet-smelling ointment
which she bore is similar to the small vials of perfume which prostitutes
sometimes wear in the Near East. Perhaps. Whatever her sin, Luke paints
the scene with sensuous, earthy, even erotic detail.

The Pharisee is shocked that Jesus allows her to touch him. The

Greek work which Luke uses for "touch" is the word *haupto* which means not only touch but also "light a fire, caress, fondle" (v. 39). Jesus appears to allow her to caress him, to fall all over him, kiss him, and in general, behave in a manner most unseemly for either the holiness of a table or the sanctity of a prophet.

Jesus asks Simon a little riddle: "A person has two debtors. One owes him a dollar; the other owes him a hundred dollars. He forgives them their debts. Now, think hard Simon; which one would be the most grateful?" (vv.41-42, author's paraphrase).

Simon answers somewhat hesitatingly, caught again in one of those penetrating, Jesus riddles. "I suppose, I expect, I guess the one who owed the larger sum."

The implication, all too clear to stuffy old Simon: She is so extravagant and reckless in her gratitude because she has been so extravagantly, recklessly forgiven. As for you, your greeting is closed, uptight, miserly, for you feel you have nothing for which to be forgiven. And there you are.

> Then those who were at table with him began to say to themselves, "Who is this, who even forgives sins?"
>
> —Luke 7:49

Who is this? Who is this who dares slap our tidy, simple categories of the saved and the damned, the sinners and the righteous? Who reveals the sin in my separation? Who breaks bread with the knowing (the woman) and unknowing (Simon) sinners? Who is this?

Doesn't Jesus know that you must be careful to make distinctions? Where would *I* be, for instance, if I did not make careful distinctions between right and wrong, good and bad, just and unjust? I make such careful judgments. I teach my children to do the same. "You have to be careful," I tell them.

When I was in high school, our church youth group participated in a fund-raising project for UNICEF, United Nations Children's Fund. Rather than do what we normally did on Halloween, we decided to help someone else for a change. We collected a considerable amount of money.

But then someone said, "My dad says that some of that money will go to countries that are communist." Well, we had to think about that. Should we be giving our money to help countries who do not like us, who may even be trying to destroy us?

"I suppose those babies do not know whether they are communist or not," observed one girl. "They only know that they are hungry!" "But after all," we said, "you have to be *careful*. 'You feed them today, you fight them tomorrow.' Isn't that how the saying goes?"

We must be careful, we reasoned. We must be careful to insure that our aid goes to the deserving, the deprived. We must be careful lest it fall into the wrong hands, into some non-Christian place. We must be careful. And so we voted to take the money and send it to our church's youth camp to help pay for a new swimming pool. You must be careful, we said.

But there was one, the Scriptures say, who was more caring then careful, one for whom my petty boundaries, distinctions, and judgments, meant little. Harlots or tax collectors, male or female, Gentile or Jew—he would eat with anybody.

Jesus was criticized because, "This man receives sinners and eats with them" (Luke 15:2). When this occurred, Jesus told his critics a little story about a lost boy. Once upon a time there was a boy who took all of his father's hard-earned savings and went out and blew it all on booze and bad women. And when the money was gone and he was hungry, the scoundrel decided to crawl back home. And you know what he got? They threw a *party*! A *party*, for heaven's sake. Karl Barth says:

> Christians who regard themselves as big and strong and rich and even dear children of God, Christians who refuse to sit with their Master at the table of publicans and sinners, are *not* Christians at all.[1]

Sinners at the Gospel Feast

Can you see why some churches have so-called "open communion"? Other churches feel that the Lord's Supper should be reserved only for the members of that congregation. Or sometimes you hear that some folk, even those within that congregation, feel that they are unworthy to commune and therefore avoid Communion. These attitudes often represent tragic misunderstandings about the Lord's Supper.

The misunderstanding is partly due to a misinterpretation of Paul's warning to the Corinthians against celebrating the Lord's Supper in "an unworthy manner" (1 Cor. 11:27). Paul's words were addressed to a specific congregation which had abused the Lord's Supper by turning it into an occasion for smug factionalism, discrimination, and selfish debauchery. He warned the Corinthians to take care to "discern the body" (v. 29), that is, to see that their fellow Christians who gather around the table are the visible body of Christ. For Paul, *body* means the church.

The Corinthians had evidently transformed this mark of unity, hospitality, community, and grace into an occasion for self-centered religious pride—the very antithesis of the Lord's Supper. So Paul tells them: You're not eating the Lord's Supper (*Kurakon diepnon*); you're eating your own supper (*idion diepnon*), literally, the "self-supper." The Corinthians' meal was a cause of separation and division; therefore, when they ate they were doing little more than eating and drinking their own destruction. The Letter of Jude criticizes those who abuse the church's meal by "looking after themselves" (v. 12).

John Wesley saw that Holy Communion was not a self-congratulatory meal for saints, but rather a life-changing meal for sinners. In theological terms, the Lord's Supper, according to Wesley, was not only a "sanctifying ordinance" for the saved; it was also a "converting ordinance" for those who are on the way to salvation. After all, reasoned Wesley, who ate with Jesus? Sinners. Some sinners were harlots, some were church leaders; some knew they were sinners, some did not. But they were all sinners, and Jesus called them all to dinner.

Therefore Wesley graciously admitted all "earnest seekers" to the Lord's table. The only requirement was a desire to meet the risen Christ.

"Come, Sinners, to the Gospel Feast," was the way an early hymn by Charles Wesley put the gracious call.

> Come, sinners, to the gospel feast;
> Let every soul be Jesus' guest;
> Ye need not one be left behind,
> For God hath bidden all mankind.
>
> Sent by my Lord, on you I call;
> The invitation is to all;
> Come, all the world! come, sinner thou!
> All things in Christ are ready now.
>
> Come, all ye souls by sin oppressed,
> Ye restless wanderers after rest,
> Ye poor, and maimed, and halt, and blind,
> In Christ a hearty welcome find.

Every time the church gathers today for the Lord's Supper, it joyfully proclaims that, wonder of wonders, Jesus still chooses the same kind of sinful, disreputable dinner companions which once got him in so much trouble.

Thank God.

CHAPTER FIVE

When You Give a Party

When one of those who sat at table with him heard this, he said to him, "Blessed is he who shall eat bread in the Kingdom of God." But he said to him, "A man once gave a great banquet, and invited many."

—Luke 14:15-16

Mind Your Manners

It was Sunday dinner at our house when I was young. The preacher had been invited to join us. As usual, we had been instructed to show our best manners and to take only the smaller pieces of fried chicken. We gathered at the table, the blessing was said, and we began to serve our plates. When the platter of chicken passed, my cousin decided to disregard parental instructions and take a chicken breast.

"Now Charles," my grandmother said politely but firmly. "You take a wing—all the pieces of chicken are good."

"Yes, m'am," he replied, "I know they're all good, so I'm just giving the preacher a chance to like them all."

Table etiquette is difficult to learn. Which fork do I eat with first? Where do I put the napkin? Where should I seat the guests? The White House employs a Chief of Protocol who has as one function the assigning of seats at important presidential dinners. Insulting a foreign diplomat by assigning the wrong seat could provoke an international crisis!

Our manners are revealing. You can tell a great deal about a person simply by watching the way that person eats. A friend of mine who is a recruiter for a large corporation always takes prospective employees to dinner. He claims that you can learn about a person's sensitivity to others, ability to include other people, and general graciousness by being with him or her at the table.

Jesus knew this. At banquets, particularly those in this kingdom of his, it's important to mind your manners. In the fourteenth chapter of Luke's gospel, Jesus proclaims a peculiar protocol for the kingdom.

A New Etiquette

> One sabbath when he went to dine at the house of a ruler who belonged to the Pharisees, they were watching him.
>
> —Luke 14:1

You have to give one thing to those fasting Pharisees, they were gluttons for punishment! They kept inviting Jesus back to dinner even when his table talk shows that he was not so pleasant a guest! Consider this sabbath meal.

A man afflicted with dropsy appears at the table (Luke 14:2f.). It is the Sabbath, and Jesus has been in trouble before because of his disregard for Sabbath customs. He asks the theologians a question: "Is it lawful to heal on the sabbath?" (Luke 14:3). In other words, "I know you think it wrong to work on the Sabbath, but is it O.K. to do *good* work on the Sabbath?"

They are silent, of course. If they answer yes, they will appear to break their own law. If they say no, they will appear cruel and insensitive. Their silence reveals the contradictions and limits of their petty, rules-and-regulations religion.

Then, perhaps observing the behavior of the guests, "how they chose the places of honor" (Luke 14:7), jockeying for prominent seats at the head table, Jesus says,

> When you are invited by anyone to a marriage feast, do not sit down in a place of honor, lest a more eminent man than you be invited by him; and he who invites you both will come and say to you, "Give place to this man," and then you will begin with shame to take the lowest place. But when you are invited, go and sit in the lowest place, so that when your host comes he may say to you, "Friend, go up higher."
>
> —Luke 14:8-10a

What kind of topsy-turvy etiquette is this? "For every one who exalts himself will be humbled, and he who humbles himself will be exalted" (Luke 14:11). Is that the way it works? Everyone is befuddled.

Then, perhaps noticing how the host has been enjoying this little exercise in getting the guests, Jesus turns to the host. "As for you," he says,

> When you give a dinner or a banquet, do not invite your friends or your brothers or your kinsmen or rich neighbors, lest they also invite you in return, and you be repaid.
> —Luke 14:12

We are talking here about a banquet. In that part of the world, a banquet was a grand occasion, a once-in-a-lifetime affair for most people. Sometimes a banquet lasted a whole week. No expense was spared to wine and dine one's guests in splendor. And Jesus says, "Don't invite your relatives and cronies because they may be able to repay the favor."

Of course they would repay the favor. What purpose would there be inviting them if they could not invite you in return? That's the whole point of invitations, right? Whom does Jesus say to invite?

> But when you give a feast, invite the poor, the maimed, the lame, the blind, and you will be blessed, because they cannot repay you.
> —Luke 14:13-14a

In other words, invite those who are utterly incapable of ever inviting you. Give an invitation to those who cannot give to you. Now everyone, host and guests, is thoroughly confused by this new brand of table manners.

Upon hearing all this talk of banquets, one of the guests hears an obvious allusion to the great messianic banquet (see chapter one) which the Messiah would spread when he comes. "Blessed is he who shall eat bread in the kingdom of God!" he shouts (v. 15).

"O how happy we shall be when the Kingdom finally comes."

"O how happy we shall be when we all get to heaven."

It's a pious little exclamation which implies that something good is going to happen to you once the Messiah comes and gets it all together and the promised banquet begins.

"Do you wish to sit at that table?" Jesus seems to ask, "Well, here's what that table looks like." And so Jesus tells them a little story, the story of the great banquet. (Luke 14:16-24).

Insiders and Outsiders

Once upon a time, a man gave a great banquet. He spared nothing to make it a grand and glorious occasion. It was to be the social event of the year. At last, when all was ready, he sent his servant to issue the invitation. "Come; for all is now ready."

Come. The thing for which you have been waiting, the event of a lifetime, the expectation of the age, is here. The time is full; the wait is over; the table is spread. Come.

But the response of those who are invited is shocking. They make excuses. Remember now, we're talking about a banquet, a once-in-a-lifetime extravagant feast for which any excuse would be regarded by the host as a grave insult.

And the excuses are ridiculous. One person has bought a house, but doesn't know where it is. Another person has bought a new car, but hasn't had the chance to drive it. Someone else has married a wife and she wants him to shampoo the carpet tonight. The excuses, particularly when one considers the value of property and livestock—and the subservience of women—in Near Eastern society, are frivolous, absurd, nonsensical, insultingly ridiculous. One can imagine that everyone is rolling in the aisles with laughter after Jesus finishes listing these ridiculous reasons for refusing the invitation.

When the servant tells this to the master, the would-be host goes through the ceiling. The master then compiles a new and radically different guest list, and says to his servant, go out quickly to the streets and lanes of the city, and bring in the poor and maimed and blind and lame (Luke 14:23, author's paraphrase).

When Matthew tells this story (22:1-10), he makes the point even more strongly by saying that the servant is told to gather "both bad and good" to fill the banquet hall (v. 10).

And they come. They come not necessarily because the poor and the maimed are better or more perceptive than the rich and the well. They come because, in their oppression, they have nowhere else to go. No other door is open to them, save this one. They come because they are hungry. Need they have a better reason?

Do you hear echoes in this unexpected guest list of Jesus' first sermon in his hometown synagogue?

> The Spirit of the Lord is upon me,
> because he has anointed me to preach good news to the poor.
> He has sent me to proclaim release to the captives

and recovering of sight to the blind,
to set at liberty those who are oppressed,
to proclaim the acceptable year of the Lord.
—Luke 4:18-19

Like the folk at Nazareth that day who heard his sermon, we naturally assume that he is talking about us when he says the acceptable year is here. After all, who is more acceptable and deserving of good news than we? But Jesus made them angry in Nazareth by reminding them that Elijah went to help a foreign widow in spite of all the good women in Israel who needed help. Elisha used his healing powers on a Syrian, in spite of all the good lepers in Israel (Luke 4:25-27). Sometimes God goes to the outsiders when the insiders refuse to listen. A prophet—an Elijah, an Elisha, or a Jesus—is rarely acceptable in his own hometown. They are not accepted because true prophets proclaim what and who is acceptable to *God,* not us.

Switching in the original Greek from the singular to the plural *you,* Jesus says to everyone, "For I tell *you,* none of those men who were invited shall taste my banquet" (Luke 14:24).

They were angry. For it is not pleasant for me—the tithing, church-going, rule-obeying, respectable lover of God that I am—to be told that God loves all those outsiders as much as he loves me. They didn't like to be told that by the hometown-boy preacher in Nazareth, nor did it go down any easier at the table in a Pharisee's house in Galilee.

So the good news of God's grace for the outsiders is coupled with inevitable bad news for us insiders. As for the rich, with our stomachs full and our fists clenched with all the possessions we regard as achievements rather than gifts, we seek no gift; therefore we are given none. Our great wealth produces its own brand of poverty. We stay home all curled up within ourselves, eating by the microwave, eyes fixed upon the TV or ourselves and our petty aches and pains, while the banquet begins without us.

Woe to you that are full now, for you shall hunger.
—Luke 6:25

All dressed up we are, with no place to go.

The Invitation

But the main theme of this great parable of the banquet is joy—the joy of being invited. The main requirement to be invited to the feast is to be hungry. And that is all of us some of the time and some of us all of the time. There is the hunger of those who have too little, and there is the hunger of those who have too much. But all hunger. The poor can testify to the indignity and the pervasive pain of hunger. The rich can tell of the skeletonlike emptiness of being fat and satisfied on the outside but starving for love and meaning on the inside.

And to all comes the great invitation.

They once asked the great missionary-evangelist, D. T. Niles, "What is 'evangelism'?" He replied that evangelism is simply one hungry beggar telling another where to find bread. Evangelism is not the well fed on TV saying sweet things to the well fed watching TV. Evangelism is not building more walls between us and them. Evangelism is not all of us gathering in our cozy little exclusive club and taking turns feeding each other. Evangelism is seeking and feeding the hungry, whatever their hunger. This is good manners.

> The lame walk, lepers are cleansed and the deaf hear, and the dead are raised up, and the poor have good news preached to them.
> —Matthew 11:5

"If this isn't evidence of the kingdom of God, what is?" Jesus wants to know.

Practically, this means that we must give more attention to how we invite people to the Lord's table. Our words and manner of inviting people to the meal should be evangelistic; that is, our invitation should feel like the good news that it is.

The traditional words of invitation are:

> Ye who do truly and earnestly repent you of your sins, and are in love and charity with your neighbors, and intend to lead a new life, following the commandments of God, and walking from henceforth in his holy ways: Draw near with faith, and take this holy Sacrament to your comfort, and make your humble confession to almighty God, devoutly kneeling.

However, lighter, more direct invitations are also possible:

> The Gifts of God for the People of God!
>
> Christ our Lord is the host at this joyous feast, and he invites all to come!

From my own observation of the way people are invited to the Lord's table, I am afraid that our ushers often do more harm than good. Our detailed, formal instructions are also a hindrance rather than a help. Rigid, militarylike, lock-step ushers are better utilized on a parade ground than at a meal. We should be hospitable and gracious in our directives. In fact, we probably give people too many directions and orders at Holy Communion. A simple, "Come to the Lord's table," allowing people to come down as the Spirit leads them and to return whenever they have been served, is enough. The invitation is to a joyous feast, not to a military, close-order drill.

Today, when people look at the church and ask it, "Are you Christ's body, or shall we look for another?" the only true test to which the church can refer is that of our Lord himself. We have to point them to our table, to that conglomeration of sick, hurting people, with the nobodies up at the head table eating like somebodies, with the outcasts invited in and being filled with good things. If this isn't church, what is?

> Day by day, attending the temple together and breaking bread in their homes, they partook of food with glad and generous hearts, praising God and having favor with all the people. And the Lord added to their number day by day those who were being saved.
> —Acts 2:46-47

CHAPTER SIX

Blessed Are the Hungry

Taking the five loaves and the two fish he looked up to heaven, and blessed and broke them, and gave them to the disciples to set before the crowd. And all ate and were satisfied.

—Luke 9:16-17*a*

Hunger

When I began teaching worship in a seminary, I asked a Roman Catholic liturgical scholar at another seminary to give me advice on how to excite Protestant seminarians about the rich possibilities for the sacrament of the Lord's Supper.

"You should begin by teaching cooking classes," he advised.

I was astonished. What did that have to do with the Lord's Supper?

"Because," he explained, "they will never lead the Eucharist with conviction until they first learn the joy of giving good food to hungry people."

Jesus would know. Jesus knew the pain of hunger and the healing possibilities in meals. Therefore, Jesus not only preached, taught, and healed; he also fed, saying, "I am the bread of life; he who comes to me shall not hunger, and he who believes in me shall never thirst" (John 6:35).

He promised his disciples at the opening of his ministry that he would confront the hunger of the world.

Blessed are you poor, for yours is the kingdom of God.
Blessed are you that hunger now, for you shall be satisfied.
　　　　　　　　　　　　　　　　　—Luke 6:20b-21a

And when he said "poor" and "hunger," that was what he meant. When Matthew records these same words in the Sermon on the Mount, they are:

> Blessed are the poor in spirit, for theirs is
> the kingdom of heaven. . . .
> Blessed are those who hunger and thirst for
> righteousness, for they shall be satisfied.
> 　　　　　　　　　　—Matthew 5:3, 6

Some people have mistakenly inferred that Matthew has somehow spiritualized the beatitudes with the additions of "poor in spirit" and "hunger and thirst *for righteousness.*" The implication is that Matthew's beatitudes, unlike those in Luke, are not really concerned with mundane, bodily needs like poverty, hunger, and thirst. They are using these phrases in a figurative sense, in a metaphorical, *spiritualized* sense.

But this interpretation fails to do justice either to Jewish concepts of the person or to the nature of poverty and hunger. No first-century Jew would understand our division of body and spirit. A person's body and a person's soul are part of a unified personality. What affects the body affects the soul and *vice versa.* We know this from our own experience. To be hungry in your stomach *is* to hunger in one's spirit. To be poor is not simply an abstracted condition of the heart or the head but is a condition which affects one's total well-being. Chronic poverty is known to have a wide array of detrimental emotional consequences. On the other hand, modern medicine is at last more fully appreciating the link between our emotional health and our physical health. To be poor in food or clothes or housing *is* to be "poor in spirit." To seek God's righteousness *is* to "hunger and thirst" after all the gifts God wills for his people.

Thus, it would be a perversion of this passage to argue (as, alas, the church has sometimes argued) that it was not real hunger or actual material poverty to which Jesus was speaking, but rather some inner, ethereal, or spiritual condition. It is just this *spiritualized* attitude which makes our worship an escape from God's will rather than a confrontation with God's will. This is the worship which Amos condemned, hearing God say:

Monstrance
Spanish — 16th century

> I hate, I despise your feasts,
> and I take no delight in your solemn assemblies.
> Even though you offer me your burnt offerings and cereal offerings,
> I will not accept them . . .
> Take away from me the noise of your songs;
> to the melody of your harps I will not listen.
>
>   —Amos 5:21-23

What is it that God wants from our worship? Something so material, so basic, as bread. Spiritual words without spiritual deeds are meaningless. Love without acts of love is not love. God says to Amos:

> But let justice roll down like waters,
> and righteousness like an everflowing stream.
>   —Amos 5:24

Nicolas Berdyaev, the Russian theologian, once said that to consider our own bread is a materialistic question; however, our neighbors' bread is a spiritual question. How tragic it is that for many people the word *spiritual* has come to mean "not real"!

The words, "Blessed are the hungry," were spoken to a people for whom poverty was a pervasive reality. Famine and the accompanying slow, agonizing death by starvation were ever-present possibilities. These words were heard by people who knew that while humanity "does not live by bread alone" (Deut. 8:3; see also Matt. 4:4), we do not live without bread either.

And it was to this poverty of body and soul, this hunger of extruding bellies and skin-and-bones deprivation that Jesus' words thundered forth, "Blessed are the poor. . . Blessed are the hungry. . . ."

In the time it takes for you to read these words, somewhere in the world, someone has closed his or her eyes and died of hunger.

He Had Compassion

It had been a hot, long, hard day. Jesus and his disciples had intended to spend the day at rest, apart from the city, but scores of people had been gathering since early morning. They pressed in upon Jesus, bringing their sick and infirm. Jesus had compassion. By midmorning he was busy healing, teaching, reaching out to the multitude. The day wore on, and still they came, still they pressed in upon him, still they sought to touch him, to look at his face, to hear his voice.

Suddenly the disciples realized it was late afternoon. In the midst of all the pushing and shoving, the waves of people, the day had slipped away. The sun was starting to descend into the Galilean hills.

"Send the crowd away," they pleaded with Jesus. "It is nearly evening. The people have nothing to eat and we are far from any village. Send the people away so that they can secure food and lodging."

But Jesus said, "Give them something to eat." What a strange command for a group which could only muster a meager five loaves and two fish from a crowd of 5000. How could he expect so little to go so far?

> Taking the five loaves and the two fish he looked up to heaven, and blessed and broke them, and gave them to the disciples to set before the crowd. And all ate and were satisfied.
>
> —Luke 9:16-17a

The story is strikingly parallel to the Old Testament account of Elisha's feeding of the hundred men from a few loaves of barley (2 Kings 4:42-44). In both stories, a small amount goes a long way to feed the hungry.

Have you ever been hungry, really hungry? In our American society, few of us have firsthand experience of the depths of hunger. Only a few still have memories of breadlines and soup kitchens and empty tin cups held out for food. But even our brief encounters with hunger can be revealing. Think about the time when you were the most hungry you have ever been. There is the gnawing emptiness in the stomach, the throbbing pain. Your head aches. You grow weak, irritable, dull. Every thought, every moment becomes fixed upon dreams of food, memories of past meals, the bliss of bread.

Human wretchedness rarely descends deeper than when in a state of hunger. Throughout the Gospels, the image of hungry humanity becomes a symbol, a vivid summary of all the wants and needs and yearnings of humanity. Thus in telling the story of the hungry 5000, Marks says Jesus looked upon those weary ones and "had compassion on them, because they were like sheep without a shepherd" (Mark 6:34).

While in no way minimizing the primary reality of physical hunger for food, the Gospels imply that the phenomenon of hunger includes, but also goes beyond, the basic need for bread. We hunger not only for bread but also for the other gifts which sustain life: love, meaning, direction, purpose, hope. The psalmist cries, "My soul thirsts . . . for the living God" (Psalm 42:2).

Mother Teresa of Calcutta, that modern saint who cares for the dying poor, notes that hunger for bread is related to other basic hungers. "We give dying people bread," she says, "because they hunger and perish not just for bread but also for love. When we hand them bread, we are also giving them love." Love which claims to love a hungry person but leaves the person hungry is meaningless.

The Holiness of Food

It is a sad commentary upon our society that our basic human hunger and emptiness are revealed not so much in our hunger caused by lack of food, but rather in our ravenous gluttony. Watch the way we eat. Food has literally gone to hell in our society of curbside rush orders, minute steaks in microwaves, instant breakfasts, and TV dinners gulped down with our eyes fixed upon the tube.

Eating has become a lonely affair for many of us. In our urbanized, technological society, most of us are cut off from the basic acts of food production and preparation. We have no sense of our food as a group product, divine gift, the result of the common labor of many hands, the gift of the good earth. The once convivial feast has been reduced to the private, individualized, plastic-packaged "McFeast."

For some time now many have noted that "we are what we eat." Our hunger for human relationships readily finds expression in patterns of eating and drinking. Caught in a daily treadmill of harried competition for daily bread, the superficiality of transitory relationships, and meaningless activity, it is little wonder that we eat as we live—hurriedly, competitively, meaninglessly.

Overeating often stems from our temptation to think that because food fills our physical void, it can fill our emotional-spiritual void as well. As we have instant oatmeal and instant potatoes, we also seek immediate gratification of all personal needs. We consume sex, friends, and experiences as if they were snacks along the way, instant soft drinks in nonreturnable cans with no messy leftovers. We gluttons die by bread alone. Our gluttony reveals the deeper contradictions, the frightening emptiness, of our hearts.

I am convinced that my own overeating, the binges I often lapse into, have a direct relation to periods of intense pressure or anxiety in my life. My weight is a kind of barometer of what is going on in me. For instance, in the summer, when I and my family are at leisure, my weight seems easier to control. In the winter, in a time of schedules and deadlines, short days and long nights, overeating is my inadequate but all-too-frequent method of coping. We are how and what we eat.

Jesus noted our anxiety about food and drink (Matt. 6:25f.; Luke 12:22f.). While his warning against anxiety over food and drink does not negate responsible concern for our sustenance, persistent worry over and preoccupation with material things gradually consume the mind. Jesus' warning about excessive food anxiety occurs immediately after the assertion, "You cannot serve God and mammon," in Matthew's Gospel.

Luke puts the warning about worry and food after the parable of the rich farmer who was obsessed by a desire to provide a large stock of goods for his future (Luke 12:13-21). The rich farmer is a man who, after having accumulated a large amount of wealth, said to himself, "Soul, take it easy, you have plenty of food laid up for yourself; relax—eat, drink and be merry" (author's paraphrase). For his attempt to gain security through the amassing of material possessions, he is called "fool." Jesus says, "Beware of all covetousness" (Luke 12:15). Beware of being misled into thinking that because we can solve some hunger with food, we can end all our hungers by stuffing our faces. Beware of thinking that because we can solve so many problems through out checkbooks, we can solve all problems that way. It is not a matter of food or money being inherently evil. It is a matter of these gifts being seductive, seducing us into a lust for godlike security. Nor is it a matter of quantity of food or money. As St. Bernard said, "A man can be a glutton over a mess of beans." It is a matter of *how* we eat rather than what or how much we eat.

In Greek, "covetousness" means "having too much." It literally means to have too much for our own good. In a consumptive, luxury-loving, pleasure-seeking age, advertising deludes us into thinking we can have the friends, peace, youth, health, and immortality we seek if we will only smoke this, drink that, smear this on our faces or under our arms. In such a climate of covetous self-gratification, we have little concern for the needs of others. We withhold from others what is rightfully theirs. We treat God's gifts of food and material possessions as if they were our personal property.

Jesus said if you have enough to have a feast, invite those who have nothing: the poor, the maimed, the lame, the blind (Luke 14:13-14). When you pray, pray for *daily* bread, not for a year's rations (Matt. 6:11).

The rich farmer is said to be laying up "treasure for himself, [but] is not rich toward God." Ravenous, covetous lust after things is seen as symptomatic of a deeper malady than mere gluttony. We evidence thereby our love for self more than God, more than love for others whom God loves. We worship wealth (Matt. 6:24), and that is really worship of ourselves.

Jesus calls for a reordering of priorities, not as a simple command to asceticism and self-denial, but as an invitation to be truly satisfied. "Seek his kingdom, and these things shall be yours as well" (Luke 12:31).

All of the preceding suggests the positive value of our daily experience of hunger. Every time your stomach growls and you feel pangs of emptiness, it reminds you that you are a creature dependent upon the gifts of a Creator and the gifts of others. You may have achieved much in life that is worthwhile and enduring, but you have not overcome your basic human need for food and for love. You are still needy, dependent, and vulnerable as far as your most basic needs are concerned. Being rich or being adult or being relatively self-sufficient does not change this basic human condition. You still hunger and thirst, you still long for love, you still grow old; your illness, your life, is still terminal.

Hunger reminds us of this. It reminds us of our own hungers. It reminds us that many of our brothers and sisters are *always* hungry. What is a temporary discomfort for us is a way of life for millions. And what about them? Hunger raises those questions in our hearts.

Beware, therefore, of any religion which claims to help us rise above or somehow overcome this basic human condition. Beware of any faith which claims to raise us so high or fill us so full that we will be exempt from the human condition. Jesus' own hungering and thirsting put him square in the middle of humanity. It does the same for us. It continues to remind us of our basic lack of fulfillment, our basic fragility, our basic dependence.

Savoring the mystery of hunger helps to whet our appetites for the mystery of food. This suggests a need to reassess the ancient art of fasting as Christians. Earlier, in chapter three, we noted the controversy surrounding the fasting of John the Baptist and friends when contrasted with the feasting of Jesus and friends. But this is not to say that fasting was absent in the experience of Jesus. He fasted forty days in the wilderness as he prayed and prepared for his ministry. He fasted after the Last Supper as preparation for his death. Jesus thus followed the ancient Jewish practice of fasting as an appropriate bodily attitude for earnest prayer and humble, empty receptivity to the will of God.

"Will you recommend fasting or abstinence, both by precept and example?" candidates for the ordained ministry are still asked in the United Methodist Church. In so doing, contemporary United Methodists follow their founder, John Wesley. Wesley's Holy Club at Oxford fasted two days a week, Wednesdays and Fridays, as did early Christians. Wesley eventually urged a weekly fast on Friday. The term *abstinence* Wesley defined as a lesser fast for times of illness, when a total fast would be unhealthful.

Wesley urged fasting as an additional means of grace which helped to discipline our comfortable life-style, to put us in touch with the basic human realities, and to "add seriousness and earnestness to our prayers." He warned against thinking that fasting was a way to win brownie points or merit badges from God. Its main value was in helping us to take our eyes off ourselves, our needs, and our achievements and to wait "with our eye singly fixed on him."

Fasting thus became an aspect of a disciplined Christian life, a life-long effort to take our minds off ourselves and to think more about God and neighbor, to be saved from our well-filled stomachs and self-filled eyes. Wesley had harsh words for the complacent, the self-satisfied. In a 1789 sermon on the causes of ineffectual Christianity, he charged:

> Many of your brethren, beloved of God, have not food to eat; they have not raiment to put on; they have not a place where to lay their head. And why are they thus distressed? Because you impiously, unjustly, and cruelly detain them from what your Master and theirs lodges in your hands on purpose to supply their wants! See that poor member of Christ, pinched with hunger . . . Meantime you have plenty of this world's goods—of meat, drink, and apparel. In the name of God, what are you doing? . . . Why do you not deal your bread to the hungry?

Through fasting we can increase our sensitivity to God and neighbor. In a culture where covetousness is virtually the basis of our economy and an expected way of life, we think we have a God-given right to as much as we can afford. Wesley's words hit hard:

> You say you can afford it! O be ashamed to take such miserable nonsense into your mouths! Never more utter such stupid cant; such palpable absurdity! Can any steward afford to be an arrant knave? To waste his Lord's good?

Stewardship and fasting go together. Hunger, even the short-term hunger of a short period of abstinence, helps to put us in touch with the poor and hungry, the ones who are reminded of their dependence and vulnerability every day—and are thereby best able to hear the good news as *their* news.[1]

As fasting prepares us for the joy of food, so silence can prepare us for the joy of the word. In Sunday worship, it is helpful to build periods of silence into the worship service—times when there is no word, no music, no sound. We must restrain our nervous habits of preacherly chatter throughout the service and musical interludes between acts of worship. How can God speak to us amid all the noise with which we fill our worship? The silence has a sort of cleansing effect upon the worshipers. It helps to increase our sensitivity, our hunger if you will, for the sound of speaking or singing. Before a prayer, before or after the scripture, before or after the sermon—all are appropriate places for periods of intentional silence. We need a few minutes to gather our thoughts and savor the silence so that we may better savor the sound, so that there is space for God to come amid the cacophony of sounds which gluts our everyday lives.

The same can be said for the ancient practice of fasting before Holy Communion. Hunger can be a positive experience. Many Christians do not eat breakfast on communion Sundays, do not "break fast." If, as we have contended, communion is essentially a body activity, then we ought to prepare our bodies. This clears body and soul for fresh experience. This whets the appetite for simpler, more basic nourishment than eggs and bacon. At least limiting breakfast on communion Sundays, going a bit light, breaking our usual weekday routine of schedules and newspapers and all the other clutter of the ordinary, helps to prepare us for the Meal.

There are wider implications. For instance, in discussing whether or not baptized children should be admitted to the Lord's table for communion, we would do well to recall the nature of this sacrament as a meal. I know of no valid biblical, theological, or historical reason for denying any baptized Christian access to this table. After all, they are in the family by virtue of their baptism. Why then should they not be allowed to eat at the family's table?

If the main requirement to be invited to eat with Jesus is simply that one be hungry, I suppose that children know as much about that as we adults. Maybe they know even more. Even the youngest Christian knows about cake at birthday parties, refreshments at school, and mama's oatmeal cookies. That's not all we hope they will one day know about the Lord's Supper—but that is certainly the place to begin knowing. Hunger has no age limit. "Let the children come to me," said Jesus (Matt. 19:14), the hungry ones of whatever age.

Pastoral care—all of the counseling, teaching, healing, sustaining, and guiding which pastors do with their parishioners for their comfort and growth—could be thought of as feeding the hungry. The first church office we read about in the New Testament is *deacon,* meaning "butler," "waiter," one who serves food and drink. Early deacons waited upon the table at the Lord's Supper and then carried the leftovers to the poor, the sick, and the imprisoned.

When his ship was in mortal danger and all were afraid, Paul urged his fellow passengers in the storm "to take some food; it will give you strength." And Paul took bread, blessed it, broke it, and ate (Acts 27:33–38). This gave his fearful companions courage. The ministry of encouragement, an important part of pastoral care, could be well served by pastors who know how to invite people to eat and be strengthened. The early church leaders called the Eucharist, "medicine for the soul."

When inviting the hungry, hospitality is important. Sometimes it is the little things which count. At the Lord's Supper, grim-faced clergy, militarylike ushers, archaic speech, miserly portions of wine in minute glasses, stingy pieces of bread—cubed, pelleted, or wafered—do not bespeak graciousness. They ask for bread; we give them a hard pellet. When evaluating communion at your church, ask yourself, "How do we make guests feel welcome at our dinner table?" What makes for hospitality at your table ought to hold true at the Lord's table—only more so. Sometimes we preach grace at communion, but our cold, rigid, robotlike, assembly-line, impersonal actions reveal exclusiveness, detachment, and insensitivity to the hungry.

As Mother Teresa reminds us, when we hand someone bread, we are also giving that person love. The simple act in the service of Holy Communion of handing someone a piece of bread is an important but often neglected part of the service. When one human being hands another human being a piece of bread, something divine happens. To place the bread at the chancel rail and have people come down and serve themselves cafeteria-style is an afront to the mystery of this moment. Communion bread should be placed in someone's hand by the server, looking into the person's eyes, calling the person's Christian (first) name if possible: "Jane, the Body of Christ, given for you." This moment should be total, personal, and sensitively done.

Lay servers should always assist the pastor in serving the bread and wine to the congregation. When lay people assist their pastor in serving communion, they are only doing on Sunday what they do throughout the week: helping their pastor feed and care for the faithful.

More than one layperson in our congregation has told me that he or she never understood Holy Communion until he or she helped serve. Jesus told us that in giving, we receive. What he said about love also applies to bread, and *vice versa.* If there are leftovers at Holy Communion, they should be taken to the sick or shut-in members as a sign of their inclusion in the Lord's table, even though they are forced to be absent. If this is not done, at least let us dispose of the leftover bread and wine in a way which shows respect for food as a gift and respect for food as a precious commodity in a hungry world. Leftovers may be passed around the congregation again until they are eaten. They may be given to someone to take home. They should not be wasted or gulped down by the celebrant while the people sit and watch. At issue here is not the holiness of communion food, but rather the holiness of all food.

Take This and Share It

They were out in the desert now. The fear and excitement of their flight from the Egyptians was over. They had made it to freedom, through the sea; now came the long, hard trek through the desert. The people became hungry, irritable, contentious. "Where will we get bread in a God-forsaken place like this?" they wanted to know. Then, wonder of wonders, the manna appears. God cares for the chosen, even in the desert, even in their griping and ingratitude. God cares for the hungry. The story of the manna in Exodus 16 is a wonderful story of God's caring for people.

But it is also a story about people caring for people. God commands the Israelites to share, to gather only what they need, to refrain from covetousness and take only enough manna for a day's hunger. Their needs are met, not lavishly, but adequately. Everyone was to have an equal share. Anyone who tried to grab and hoard the food found that in the hoarding the food became spoiled. The story, so full of lessons for us, is Israel's wistful look back to the desert years when life seemed simpler and more basic, when there were no class distinctions and people shared what they had. Perhaps you remember such a time in your own past.

When we see food as a surprising, undeserved gift of God to sustain us for the journey, the food becomes holy. When we grab and hoard, we not only impoverish others, we spoil it for ourselves. The hungry of the world will not sit by idly and watch their children starve while we and our children indulge in gluttony. We cannot lay up for ourselves military and economic treasures which can make us secure for this coming judgment. There is blasphemy in a former United States Secretary of Agriculture speaking of "using food as a weapon" to get other nations to do what we want. Food is not a possession, nor a weapon. It is a gift. Of course, we have used so many of God's other gifts as weapons in vain attempts to win security for ourselves, why not use food?

When Jesus compares himself with manna, as he often does in John's Gospel, when he calls himself bread for the world, he surely implies that you cannot receive the gift that he offers without receiving it through sharing.

In the midst of a famine, if a person comes upon a piece of bread and takes the bread, gives thanks for the bread and eats it, that is a meal.

In the midst of a famine, if a person comes upon a piece of bread and takes the bread, gives thanks for the bread and then shares half of it with someone who has none, that is a *sacrament.* "As you did it to one of the least of these my brethren, you did it to me" (Matt. 25:40).

As for me, I am grateful that when Jesus came proclaiming the advent of his kingdom, he did not begin with sermons about reconciliation, atonement, justification, redemption or any other big, abstract, high-sounding words. He began by pointing to our stomachs, to that gnawing, unsatisfied, emptiness within. And then he invited us to dinner.

Then, having fed us, he charged us to feed others. In spite of our inadequacies, cowardice, greed, and fears, he told us, "Feed my sheep" (John 21:15-17). He points us away from our loaded tables and full hearts and (in spite of our limitations as disciples and providers) points us to the hungry, saying, "Give them something to eat." He takes up the cup of salvation and says, "Take this, and divide it among yourselves" (Luke 22:17).

And wonder of wonders, when we dare to do what he says, like the boy with five loaves and two fish, it is enough.

> Then the King will say to those at his right hand, "Come, O blessed of my Father, inherit the kingdom prepared for you. . . . For I was hungry and you gave me food."
>
> —Matthew 25:34-35a

CHAPTER SEVEN

In the Upper Room

You are those who have continued with me in my trials; as my Father appointed a kingdom for me, so do I appoint for you that you may eat and drink at my table in my kingdom, and sit on thrones.

—Luke 22:28-30

At the Passover

Of all the memorable meals in the Gospels, the most memorable is the meal in the upper room (Luke 22:7-38, Matt. 26:17-19, Mark 14:12-16). Luke says that it was a Passover meal, a feast in which Israel celebrated its liberation from slavery and remembered its identity: a redeemed, loved, delivered, liberated, chosen people of God. The Passover was therefore a time of great joy, feasting, and thankful remembrance.

For the disciples of Jesus who gathered with their master in the upper room, the meal was also an occasion for redemption, liberation, and deliverance. Looking back, the disciples would come to see this meal (the only one we have mentioned where Jesus was the host) as a sign of their "pass over" from death to life, from slavery to freedom.

Four Conversations

In the midst of the raucous joy of thousands of pilgrims who have flocked to Jerusalem to celebrate the Passover, the dark currents which now swirl around Jesus and his disciples are a stark contrast. Luke says the members of the religious establishment "were seeking how to put him to death" (Luke 22:2). Judas had struck a deal with Jesus' enemies to betray him. The storm clouds were gathering.

It is in this context of contrasting light and dark that Jesus and his disciples gathered in an upper room, the second floor room for a home. The hour of the meal was sometime soon after sundown as the last light of day had fled from the city.

As they sat at the table, Jesus opened the meal by predicting, "I shall not eat it [again] until it is fulfilled in the kingdom of God" (v. 16). In other words, he would not eat the Passover again until he eats the promised great banquet in the kingdom. After this meal, the time for fasting and sorrow would come. The party was almost over.

Following Jewish mealtime customs, Jesus takes the cup and gives thanks over the wine. This is the "cup of blessing" (see 1 Cor. 10:16). After the opening prayer of thanks, the cup is divided among the disciples with another prediction of fasting: "from now on I shall not drink of the fruit of the vine until the kingdom of God comes" (Luke 22:18).

Now he takes the loaf and breaks it. This is the meal itself. At this time the Passover lamb would be eaten. (The very poor must content themselves with only bread for the meal.) A prayer of thanksgiving is offered for the bread. After this blessing, the bread is broken and passed around the table. This is all familiar Jewish table ritual. But Jesus adds some strikingly unfamiliar words: *This is my body.* What can he mean?

We miss the full significance of this meal if we focus only upon the so-called "words of institution." The richness of the upper room experience goes beyond, "This is my body." Unfortunately, in the Middle Ages and in the liturgies of the Reformation, we focused upon those words of Christ at the exclusion and neglect of his other words at this meal. But the significance of this meal in the upper room is similar to the significance of all the other meals with Jesus which we have discussed—in the table talk, in the stories, in the nature of those who are at the table with Jesus.

The table talk in the upper room can be divided into four main conversations:

No sooner than the meal and the table talk began, Jesus drops the bombshell: "But behold the hand of him who betrays me is with me on the table" (Luke 22:21). The table is in disarray. "Is it I?" each asks. This is the moment Leonardo da Vinci depicts in his famous painting, *The Last Supper.* Note that all the disciples are uncertain as to who will betray him, for "they began to question one another, which of them . . . would do

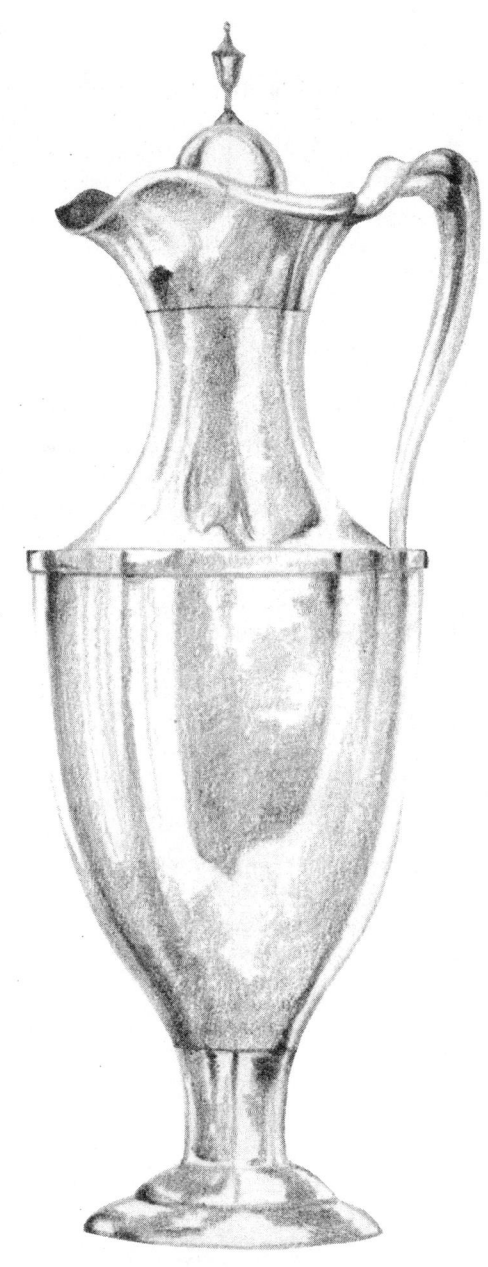

Silver Flagon
King's Chapel, Boston
Made by Paul Revere, 1798

this" (v. 23). Anyone at the table might betray him. No one was secure from temptation.

Then a dispute arises among all the disciples over which one will be greatest in the kingdom (verses 24-27). In the other gospels, this argument occurs at other places (Mark 9:34, John 13:3-16). Luke, dramatic genius that he was, places the argument here. By placing the dispute over greatness in the upper room, Luke shows that the disciples have absolutely no understanding of who Jesus is as the suffering servant, nor any understanding of what his kingdom is as the kingdom of the poor and the outcast.

Here they were, the men who heard his sermons and teaching, arguing, "When we get him elected Messiah, who will be secretary of state?"

The argument over greatness had occurred before, back at the very beginning:

> And an argument arose among them as to which one of them was the greatest. But when Jesus perceived the thought of their hearts, he took a child and put him by his side, and said . . . to them ". . . he who is least among you all is the . . . great."
>
> —Luke 9:46-48

Now, as if referring them back to that day, he says, "let the greatest among you become as the youngest, and the leader as one who serves. . . . I am among you as one who serves" (Luke 22:26-27).

In the rock musical *Jesus Christ Superstar,* this scene is vividly portrayed. As Christ serves food to the disciples, as he prepares for his humiliating death upon the cross, the disciples drink more and more wine and begin to sing a song to the effect, "Look at me. Look at all my trials and tribulations. Look at how much I've suffered and all that I've sacrificed. Maybe someday they will write a book about me."

The scene is comic and tragic. In their argument, the disciples show they still do not understand about this new kingdom. They still think Jesus is going to be a military overlord, a political potentate, a reward-giving, religious entrepreneur, preaching, "something good is going to happen to you." They are still looking for a miracle worker who turns stones to bread (Matt. 4:3-4).

As they squabble over who is the greatest, Jesus becomes the deacon (the butler or waiter) and waits upon the table. When John tells the story in his gospel (chapter 13), he drives the point even further by having Jesus not only serve the disciples but also wash their feet. In so doing, Jesus acts out the kind of lowly servanthood which typifies both his ministry and life in his kingdom.

And yet it is to these misunderstanding, ignorant, confused, self-centered ones that Jesus promises seats of honor in the coming kingdom. Even though their ignorance and betrayal show that they don't deserve it, he goes to prepare a banquet for *them*. This is the good news.

> You are those who have continued with me in my trials; as my Father appointed a kingdom for me, so do I appoint for you that you may eat and drink at my table in my kingdom, and sit on thrones judging the twelve tribes of Israel.
>
> —Luke 22:28-30

In the gathering dark amid the sin, ignorance, and betrayal—the light of his graciousness shines all the more brightly. This good news contrasts with the generally bad news within the now darkened upper room. The good news: these are the sinners with whom he chooses to share food and drink; these are the sinners whom he serves; these are the sinners for whom he goes to prepare the great banquet.

The third major dialogue focuses upon Simon Peter (22:31-33). "Satan demanded to have you," says Jesus to Peter (v. 31). The "you" here switches in mid-sentence from singular to plural, indicating that Jesus is speaking not only to Peter but to the others as well. Satan has entered the entire company; any may betray Jesus; no one is safe from the tempter's snare.

But once again, Jesus prays for these tempted ones (v. 32). Peter declares "Lord, I am ready to go with you to prison and to death" (v. 33). But Jesus knows Peter will be unable to stand fast in the coming fury: "I tell you, Peter, the cock will not crow this day, until you three times deny that you know me" (v. 34). And yet this is the disciple for whom he prays, "When you have turned again, strengthen your brethren" (v. 32).

Now occurs a fourth and final dialogue concerning swords (vv. 35-38). It is a strange conversation. Jesus asks his disciples, "When I sent you out with no purse or bag or sandals, did you lack for anything?" (v. 35). Then Jesus tells them if they have swords, to get ready to use them.

> They said, "Look, Lord, here are two swords." And he said to them, "It is enough."
>
> —Luke 22:38

This is all strange, for it seems odd that Jesus would ask his disciples to carry swords. It's particulary strange in light of what happens a few moments later. When the authorities come to seize Jesus and the disciples use their swords, Jesus harshly rebukes them. He says, "No more of this!" (v. 51).

Some scholars suggest that the talk about having swords might be Jesus' way of saying that the time of struggle has at last begun and the disciples must arm themselves against hostility—but not literally to arm themselves with swords, for that would be a violation of the nature of the kingdom.

Other scholars speculate that the two swords may relate to the two witnesses which Old Testament law required to convict someone of a capital crime. If this is correct, Jesus is saying in effect, "Do you have evidence that you have disobeyed me?"

Yes, there is evidence. Two swords are present. Did not Jesus clearly tell them (Luke 10:4) that they were to take nothing with them when they followed him? No purse, no bag, no sandals, and surely by implication, no swords. The presence of the two swords is visible, conclusive proof that the disciples failed to do what Jesus told them to do.

Just in case this Jesus movement did not work out, the disciples reasoned, just in case his power proved insufficient, just in case the going got rough—a couple of swords were taken along for insurance. Their desire for security through the sword is testimony to their basic disobedience and earns them their master's rebuke.

And they go out to the Mount of Olives where Jesus prays and urges his disciples to "pray that you may not enter into temptation" (Luke 22:40, 46). But, alas, they sleep. And when at last the soldiers and captors come to seize him, both the disciples and the captors have swords. They both participate in the powers of darkness. There is no difference between the actions and weapons of the disciples and those of the captors.

"No more of this!" commands Jesus as he is led away to die while the disciples flee into the darkness.

It is a sad story. As Jesus is led away toward his trial and death the next day, his twelve best friends forsake him and flee. Acted out before us is the same sad tragedy of fear, self-centeredness, ignorance, cowardice, and betrayal which we have played out time and again in our history, time and again in our own lives. We, like the disciples, try to get our act together. We want to be faithful. We intend to be brave. We mean to stick by our friends and stand up for the right. But in the end, when the going gets rough, when there is a high price to be paid, when we must act upon our good intentions, we flee into the safe anonymity of the gathering dark.

Good News Amid the Bad

And yet behind the sadness of it all, there is an underlying joy in the events in the upper room. In this story, as in the other stories of meals, there is the good news. It is the good news of a savior who eats and drinks with sinners. Even in the midst of their sin, Jesus promises the disciples a prominent place at the banquet table in the kingdom. He goes to get things ready for these sinners who also happen to be disciples.

So it was a Passover, this Maundy Thursday meal in the upper room, a passover from bondage to freedom. A new covenant was being ratified that night, a covenant sealed by Christ's love for us even unto death. Like the covenant of old, the new covenant would be at God's initiative, not ours. We could not keep faithful to the end, so God remained faithful to us. We could not stand beside God to the end, so Jesus took his place beside us. Even as our love faltered and stumbled, God's love endured.

Judas was not the only betrayer that night, not the only one to betray him with a kiss, to forsake him even as he was pretending to embrace him. Matthew ends the story, "Then all the disciples forsook him and fled" (26:56). All.

I'm glad Judas was at the table with him that dark Thursday night, and Peter and all the rest. For if they had not been there then, I don't know how I could dare, my unfaithfulness being what it is, to come to the Lord's table on Sunday morning.

Christ our passover is sacrificed for us: therefore let us keep the feast.
— 1 Corinthians 5:7b-8a, KJV

CHAPTER EIGHT

Proclaiming Death

For as often as you eat this bread and drink the cup, you proclaim the Lord's death until he comes.
—1 Corinthians 11:26

Table or Altar?

It was the same old thing. The disciples had asked him before; they would ask him again.

"Grant us [the sons of Zebedee asked] to sit, one at your right hand and one at your left, in your glory" (Mark 10:37). As in the upper room (Luke 22:24-27), they sought rewards, glorious results, and prestigious payoffs for their discipleship. Surely this was not asking too much from Jesus. After all, they had "left everything and followed him" (Luke 5:11).

Jesus responds, "You do not know what you are asking. Are you able to drink the cup that I drink, or to be baptized with the baptism with which I am baptized?" (Mark 10:38). This "cup" of which he speaks, this "baptism," would be revealed at Golgotha. He was speaking of his death.

The disciples looked for glory; Jesus led them toward death. I thought of words from Thomas a Kempis in *The Imitation of Christ:*

> Jesus now hath many lovers of His celestial kingdom:
> > but few bearers of His Cross.
> He hath many who are desirous of consolations:
> > but few of tribulation.
> He findeth many companions of His table:
> > but few of His abstinence.

All desire to rejoice with Him:
> few wish to endure anything for Him.

Many follow Jesus to the breaking of bread:
> but few to the drinking of the cup of His Passion.

Many reverence His miracles:
> few follow the shame of His Cross.

We are like that. We are all bound for glory but we do not want inconvenient detours along the way. We want to sit at the great heavenly banquet, but when the cup of sorrow comes our way we plead, "Let this cup pass from me." We are like that.

Thus a friend of mine says that he is skeptical of my emphasis upon the Lord's Supper as a meal, as a time of fellowship and life, to the exclusion of some of our former stress upon Holy Communion as a time of sacrifice and death. "At Holy Communion, are we coming to the table or to the altar?" he asks.

In recent years, we have recovered the ancient emphasis upon the table. The old altars, which were pushed against the back wall of the sanctuary and placed on high steps away from the people in the Middle Ages, have been converted to small tables, brought out into the light, set in the midst of the congregation, as they were in the early church. My friend questions some of this. He does not mind the recovery of the Lord's Supper as a meal, but he wonders if, beneath our current emphasis upon the fellowship and joy of the sacrament, we may be avoiding some of its more threatening, more challenging implications.

He reminds me that a table is more accessible than an altar. The table is a place of linen napkins and fine silver, of merriment and polite conversation broken only by the tinkling of knives and forks. The table is a place of good manners, warm hospitality, and a receptive and close God. The altar, on the other hand, is a mysterious place of sacrifice, of life-and-death matters. Here stands a priest in the holy of holies, knife in hand, preparing to slit the throat of some cow or goat. The altar is enmeshed in the screams of dying animals, blood trickling down the marble steps. There is talk of sin and death and sacrifice before a distant, demanding God.

But even the table, for all its character as a place of joy and etiquette, is a place of sacrifice. From whence did the chicken come which your family ate last night for dinner? In our world of air-conditioned, piped-in music, cellophaned, antiseptic supermarkets, we moderns forget that something had to die, blood had to be spilt, to enable us to sit down to Sunday dinner. The life-giving food is not on our table without the death of something and the sacrifice of someone.

In a bygone day when my grandmother prepared dinner by going into the backyard, capturing a hen, wringing its neck, then plucking and dressing it—one could not so easily escape the ever-present reality of blood and sacrifice, of cost and death, behind our pleasant times of food and conversation.

Not only in our eating and drinking but also in our religion there is a tendency to avoid or deny the realities of pain, suffering, death, and cost which lie behind our hopes of healing, comfort, reward, and bliss. In the words of Thomas a Kempis,

> Many follow Jesus to the breaking of bread:
>   but few to the drinking of the cup of His Passion.
> Many reverence His miracles:
>   few follow the shame of His Cross.

I am thinking now of a folder which I received recently in the mail. It was sent to me by an "evangelist" in Arizona assuring me that God has something good to give me. It asked whether I needed a new car or if I were suffering from financial problems. The folder promised a plan through which God would bless me beyond my wildest dreams. For an initial investment of ten dollars I can begin to receive all these good things from God—or so the folder says. The folder is full of testimonials from people who received this or that, all because they prayed and sent money to this man and his organization. "Jesus Christ is the best deal a person ever had," exclaims one woman from the midwest. She was given a promotion in her job and a substantial raise—all because she became a Christian and started sending money to this evangelist. I heard of a new book by another evangelist which says it all—*How to Stay on Top*.

But let me not be too severe with these "evangelists" and their followers. The same self-serving attitude can be found in my church, in my sermons, in my attitudes as well. I may not expect Jesus to give me a new car or a raise in pay, but I certainly expect good health, a happy marriage, and devoted children as fringe benefits of my faith. Most of the benefits I offer my parishioners are psychological rather than material (peace, joy, fulfillment, freedom from worry, etc.), but they are still promised as pay-offs for following Christ.

I may not be promising even so mild a payoff as joy, but I do subtly assure them that, whatever discipleship means, it does not mean risk, cost, or pain. Wherever we are following Christ, we assure ourselves on Sunday morning—in our padded pews in air-conditioned sanctuaries, with soft-voiced preachers and soothing choirs—we assure ourselves that we are not following him anywhere so inconvenient and dangerous as Calvary.

We have signed on for the glory of it all, not for the pain. Let this cup pass from us. It is fine to sit with Jesus at the table, but let some other lambs than us be led with him to the slaughter. Let's stick to the table and keep our conversation light and cheerful, talk about all the good things God is going to give us, expect a miracle, and smile. The altar is for brass candlesticks and bouquets of carnations—not for our Lord, not for *us*.

Let This Cup Pass from Us

Every time I despair and lose hope for the churches I serve, I think of the churches Paul served and then I take heart. Things may get bad around here from time to time. We may have our squabbles and disagreements. But at least things have never been as bad as they were in First Church Corinth!

We do not know the precise nature of the Corinthians' troubles, but from Paul's letter to them we know that the Christians at Corinth were bitterly divided.

Paul says, "It has been reported to me by Chloe's people that there has been quarreling among you, my brethren" (1 Cor. 1:11). Not only that, "It is actually reported that there is immorality among you" (5:1a). Bickering, self-righteousness, boasting, litigation between Christians, and sexual immorality have fractured the church at Corinth into a dozen feuding factions. Paul appeals to them, using a Passover image. He reminds them that even a little leaven or yeast goes a long way in a lump of dough:

> Do you know that a little leaven ferments the whole lump of dough? Cleanse out the old leaven that you may be fresh dough, as you really are unleavened. For Christ, our paschal lamb, has been sacrificed. Let us, therefore, celebrate the festival, not with the old leaven, the leaven of malice and evil, but with the unleavened bread of sincerity and truth.
>
> —1 Corinthians 5:6–8

The "festival" of which Paul speaks is probably the Sunday meal which Paul calls "the Lord's Supper." Evidently there must have been a fair amount of the "old leaven of malice and evil" when the Corinthians broke bread. Their factionalism is nowhere more apparent than when they gather for worship.

He tells the Corinthians that when they gather "it is not for the better but for the worse" (11:17b). "I hear that there are divisions among you; and I partly believe it," he says (11:18b). Paul's anger rises; his words become more harsh as he thinks what the Corinthians have done to the meal.

> When you meet together, it is not the Lord's Supper that you eat. For in eating, each one goes ahead with his own meal, and one is hungry and another is drunk. What! Do you not have houses to eat and drink in? Or do you despise the church of God and humiliate those who have nothing? What shall I say to you? Shall I commend you in this? No, I will not.
>
> —1 Corinthians 11:20-22

Paul then recounts the tradition of the institution of this holy meal in the upper room:

> For I received from the Lord what I also delivered to you, that the Lord Jesus on the night when he was betrayed took bread. . . . For as often as you eat this bread and drink the cup, you proclaim the Lord's death until he comes.
>
> —1 Corinthians 11:23, 26

Rather than proclaiming the Lord's death, the Corinthians through their self-centeredness are proclaiming their own sinfulness. Paul regards this as a perversion of the Lord's Supper.

> Whoever, therefore, eats the bread or drinks the cup of the Lord in an unworthy manner will be guilty of profaning the body and blood of the Lord. Let a man examine himself, and so eat of the bread and drink of the cup. For anyone who eats and drinks without discerning the body eats and drink judgment upon himself.
>
> —1 Corinthians 11:27-29

Paul instructs them in Christian table manners: "When you come together to eat, wait for one another" (11:33).

What was the root of the Corinthians' problems? Biblical scholars suggest that the Corinthians were confused about the Lord's Supper. They were guilty of "profaning the body and blood of the Lord" because they ate and drank without "discerning the body." The image *body* is used here the same way Paul uses it throughout this letter and others. He is calling the *church* the "Body of Christ." The Corinthians in their bickering and factionalism "despise the church of God." One runs ahead and stuffs himself while another member starves. This is less than the communion which the meal is meant to be.

A major source of trouble is the Corinthians' misunderstanding and misuse of "spiritual gifts" (12:1f.). Inspired people in the church are speaking in tongues, healing, prophesying, and doing other good things, but they are doing them in conceited, arrogant ways—"Me graduate school Christian; You kindergarten Christian." Paul tells them just as one body has many members with different functions, so the Body of Christ (the church) has many members which should use their gifts, not for personal achievement, not for individual advancement, not to put others down, but for the good of all.

In spite of all their spiritual gifts, the Corinthians lack the one gift that enables them to be the Body of Christ: *love*.

If I speak in the tongues of men and of angels, but have not love, I am a noisy gong or a clanging cymbal.
—1 Corinthians 13:1

Perhaps the Corinthians confused the Lord's Supper with the sacred meals in their old pagan religions. In the mystery cults, sacred food was eaten in an attempt by the person to achieve personal immortality by gulping down this supposedly magical substance. Holy bread and holy wine were consumed, and sometimes blood was drunk, in hopes of filling the body with life-preserving, magic food. In other words, the purpose of these sacred meals in the pagan cults was to eat lots of holy food in order to be fulfilled, to be saved from death and evil, to live forever.

It is understandable that Corinthian Christians assumed that Christian talk about eating and drinking the body and blood of Christ meant the same magic immortality meal which they had enjoyed in the pagan cults. So let's rush ahead of the poor, grab as much holy food as we can, cure our own aches and pains, and live forever—so they thought.

But Paul tells them they thought wrong. He reminds them that their forebears ate the sacred food (manna) in the wilderness. But because of their disobedience and contentiousness, they were condemned. The supernatural food alone did not save them (1 Cor. 10:1-5). The Lord's Supper is not some personal, magical, mystery meal. It is not a time for selfish debauchery. "For as often as you eat this bread and drink the cup, you proclaim the Lord's death until he comes" (1 Cor. 11:26). In other words, Paul counters the Corinthians' spiritualistic, self-centered excesses by referring them to Jesus, the death of Jesus to be exact. The cross.

The real Jesus was rejected; he suffered and died. His obedience to God ended upon a cross. Why should the Corinthians expect some magical bypassing of this scandalous cross? What makes them think that discipleship leads to rewards, benefits, and payoffs for us as individuals rather than service to others?

So Paul says in his opening remarks to the proud, conceited, self-serving Corinthians,

> When I came to you brethren, I did not come proclaiming to you the testimony of God in lofty words or wisdom. For I decided to know nothing among you except Jesus Christ *and him crucified.*
> —1 Corinthians 2:1-2 (my emphasis)

Paul countered the Corinthians' self-serving religion by reminding them of the self-giving of Jesus. The Corinthians seek gifts. Christ gave himself. There is an ethical dimensional to the Lord's Supper. Paul preached to the Corinthians not about healing, immortality, rewards, or any of the other things that infatuated them. He preached to them about what Jesus did. He preached about the cross. He preached about death.

The Lord's Supper proclaims this death, says Paul. Jesus ate the Last Supper before he went out to die. That meal occurred "on the night when he was betrayed" (1 Cor. 11:23). He ate in the midst of betrayal, cowardice, greed, and the self-seeking faith of his disciples. All the sin and evil of the world was there that night with him at the table.

All of our illusions about ourselves, the lies by which we live, the big and little conceits with which we try to tell ourselves that we are basically nice people who are becoming nicer, that we are making progress, that we can save ourselves by ourselves, that we can serve God without risk of pain or cost—all of this was disproved in the upper room and on the cross.

Jesus Christ was condemned and crucified by everything that was deemed respectable in his day—religious leaders, government authority, even the democracy of the crowd which wanted Barabbas rather than Christ. The cross accuses our alleged righteousness and calls it a sham. We are most sinful precisely in those high, enthusiastic moments when we, like the Corinthians, think that we are saved, redeemed, pure, and good. It is in those moments of self-delusion about our divinity that we are capable of our demonic worst.

The Lord's Supper proclaims to all that the cross is not optional equipment for Christians. The way of obedience and faithfulness invari-

The Church of the Resurrection
Amsterdam

ably leads to the cross, the world being what it is. If we would follow Christ, we must take up the cross and follow. Evil must be confronted rather than masked by grinning, successful Christians. Injustice, oppression, prejudice, war, famine, sickness, the everyday big and little cruelties which we inflict upon others, those which others inflict upon us, and those which we inflict upon ourselves must be fought.

The Lord's Supper proclaims that our Lord entered the flesh. Jesus lived in this world, not some other fantasy world. He lived and hungered and suffered and died—as we must. He confronted evil on its own turf. He yoked himself in solidarity with this whole suffering, sinful mass of dying humanity. He

> emptied himself, taking the form of a servant, being born in the like-ness of men. And being found in human form he humbled himself and became obedient unto death, even death on a cross.
> —Philippians 2:7-8

He "emptied himself." As for us, like the Corinthians before us, we seek to fill ourselves, stuff ourselves full of ourselves, cure all our aches and pains, and live forever—to the neglect of everybody else. This is not the faith which Jesus proclaimed.

Our sin is a consequence of our inward idolatry, our worship of our own selves. From here flow all our moral problems of prejudice against others, dishonesty, and aggression. All of these sins are the result of the sin of worshiping something other than God—namely, ourselves—and of hoping to shed our creatureliness and be gods rather than seeking the security which only God can give. This is sin. It leads to death.

For Paul, the answer to our sin is the cross. On the cross we see the prototype for our transformation. Jesus was obedient there—obedient to God, obedient even unto death. There he gave himself for us. That self-giving becomes the model, the vision, the way. As Paul says, to eat in selfishness and idolatrous self-centeredness is to fail to "discern the body," to eat and drink in an "unworthy manner," to do to others the very opposite of what Christ did for us.

Paul says we are saved or judged at the table by our willingness to become vulnerable and bear the cross and to enter into the death of Christ. Without that death, there will be no life.

In the end, the angel says to the fat, suburban, complacent, successful church, "I know your works; you have the name of being alive, and you are dead" (Rev. 3:1). To the cruciform churches of Poland, South Korea, Angola, or the inner city, the angel says, "I know that you have but little power, and yet you have kept my word and have not denied my name" (Rev. 3:8).

As Often as You Do This

As often as we come forward to the Lord's Supper, we come not only to a table but also to an altar. Our sin and death are real. They cannot be explained away or avoided. They must be confronted. We are on the way with Jesus to the cross. We keep wishing the way led to the joy of Palm Sunday or to bypass it all and head straight for Easter light. But the way leads also to a dark Good Friday.

Too often, American evangelical Christianity presents the good news of Christ as the solution for all human problems, the fulfillment of all our wants, a good way to make basically good people even better. But the cross suggests that the good news is the beginning of problems, the turning away from our quest for self-fulfillment, the ultimate mocking of our delusions of goodness. Nothing less than death will do. Nothing less than deadly, painful, full-scale conversion—turning around from ourselves toward God and others.

Christianity is a thing of great comfort. But it does not begin in comfort; it begins in some pain. We cannot ask for the comfort before we face the cross. The cross reminds us that God gains victories through pain rather than through force, through self-giving rather than self-seeking. Our victories come the same way.

The Lord's Supper is not some magical medicine we take to exempt outselves from the hard facts of life in this world. But it can provide a way of dealing with those hard facts. No prayers of a television evangelist, no "prayer cloth" from Arizona, no holy oil, no holy water, no holy food exempts us from the possibilities of pain, sickness, injustice, or death. To seek such exemption is to cease to follow the way of Christ.

But at the table, before the altar, even our most painful times are redeemed because our Lord saves through suffering. The self-giving of God in Christ in the sacraments is a self-giving even unto death.

As a friend lay in her hospital bed, her body wracked by the last stages of terminal cancer, she said to me through her pain, "I couldn't take it except that I know that *he* has been through this and worse before me."

Therein is our hope. Without the cross, our faith wouldn't be a comfort to anybody. What would you say to the terminal cancer victim? What would you say to the mother of a starving child in an Ethiopian desert? What would you say to the eighty-year-old resident of a shoddy nursing home for the elderly? "Smile, God Loves You!" No, I hope not.

You can say that our God has been there before, in the pain, in the darkness, in the death, that Christ has come through it and that all is well.

And even this is little comfort if the church is not willing to take up the crosses of those whom the world crucifies today. Christ is rarely to be found among the "successful." Wherever a cross is raised in our world, he is there with the crucified. We must be there, too, proclaiming the presence of the crucified God. This graffito appeared on the wall of the room where the youth met for church school: *I Asked Jesus How Much He Loved Me. And He Stretched Out His Hands And Died.*

We are recipients of many blessings because others have suffered for us, have given themselves for us. Vicarious suffering is all around us. The coal miner laboring in the depths of the earth provides your warmth and light. We live in a free country because patriots died to purchase our freedom. The church endures on the blood of martyrs; someone labored to put bread on your table this morning. Holy Communion reminds us that we live because Christ died.

> He has borne our griefs and
> carried our sorrows . . .
> he was wounded for our transgressions,

> he was bruised for our iniquities;
> upon him was the chastisement that
> made us whole,
> and with his stripes we are healed.
>   —Isaiah 53:4*a*, 5

In a hurting world where evil still runs rampant and injustice still sends good people to the cross, we Christians do have something to preach. We, like Paul before us, preach Christ and him crucified.

In a world where everyone looks for a cushion rather than a cross, where religious hucksters tell us we can have power, prestige, position, breakfast at the White House, and heaven, too—we, like Paul, preach Christ and him crucified.

The bread and wine had been offered for Communion and I stood behind the Lord's table with my arms outstretched to pray the prayer of thanksgiving. "Look, Mommie," one of our younger members exclaimed. "He's trying to look like Jesus on the cross."

It's not a bad thing to say about a Christian: She's trying to look like Jesus on the cross.

To a death-denying, satisfaction-seeking, self-serving world, as often as we break bread and gather at the table, we "proclaim the Lord's death until he comes" (1 Cor. 11:26).

CHAPTER NINE

When He Was at Table with Them

Then they told what had happened on the road, and
how he was known to them in the breaking of the
bread.

—Luke 24:35

The Meal at Emmaus

The day was ending. Now shadows grew longer. The sun had
begun its descent into the West. Two somber figures trudged along a
dusty road—the road leading from Jerusalem to an insignificant little
place called Emmaus.

The eyes of the two travelers were fixed upon their feet as they
walked. They talked together in low, solemn tones. Suddenly they
became aware of a third person, a man who now walked beside them as
they began their ascent up yet another hill.

"What are you talking about?" he asked the two travelers.

They stopped at the peak of the hill, catching their breath, leaning
upon their walking sticks, answering the stranger without lifting their eyes
to his face. "Are you the only one in town who doesn't know what has
happened in Jerusalem this weekend?"

"What things?" asked the stranger.

"Those things concerning Jesus of Nazareth, the man we followed,
a prophet of mighty words and deeds. The establishment put him to
death. We had hoped he would be the one to redeem Israel, the Messiah

who would save us. But what can you do? You can't fight city hall, as they say. He is gone. It was good while it lasted, but we didn't get him elected king. Death has the final word. He is gone."

"Some of our women," added the other disciple, "came running in this morning saying they could not find his body at the tomb. They even claim to have seen angels who said he was alive. But what do they know?"

"O foolish men!" exclaims the stranger. "So slow of heart are you!"

And for the rest of that late afternoon, until the sun was but a faint glow in the west, they talked as they walked, the stranger interpreting the scriptures to them along the way.

At last they came to the little village of Emmaus. The mysterious stranger now bid them farewell. But the disciples begged him to stay. "The day is over; night has come; stay with us at the inn."

That evening at the table, the stranger took the loaf of bread, held it in his hands, blessed it, thanking God for the bread and for the meal. He broke it in half and gave it to them. At last, at the table, at the meal, their eyes were opened and they saw who the stranger was. He vanished from their sight.

Kicking back their chairs, bounding out the door, they did not walk but ran back toward Jerusalem. There they found the rest of the disciples and breathlessly told them how Christ was known to them in the breaking of the bread.

They had trudged to Emmaus that Sunday thinking that the party was over. At the table, to their delighted surprise, they saw that they were wrong. The party had just begun.

Resurrection Meals

Why did the disciples see the risen Christ at Emmaus only in the breaking of the bread? Even when Christ walked beside them, even when he rebuked them, even when he interpreted the scriptures to them, they were unable to see.

What was there in the breaking of the bread that made him known to them? Did his presence at the table trigger memories of past meals? We do not know. We only know that here at Emmaus, the table once again became a place of disclosure, recognition, and revelation. Once again the table became a place of worship.

Once again the disciples (the church) gather on Sundays. They are despondent, defeated, dejected. Why shouldn't they be so? Whenever disciples (the church) gather and glance backward at our record of achievement or progress, that record is dismal. Good Fridays seem more in tune with reality than Easter Sundays. After all, we are sensible people who know that this is the way things are. You can't fight city hall. It was a good campaign while it lasted but we didn't get him elected Messiah. What can anybody do?

Modern humanity, having raised so many crosses in our own day, easily understands why Jesus was hanged on a cross in his day. Wars, concentration camps, 6,000,000 Jews murdered, thousands starving, refugees, terrorism—we know that in the end the good get it. We know the suffering our evil causes. We know. But what can anybody do about it? There are so few of us disciples, and we are so weak, so unfaithful. What can anybody do?

But then, in the midst of our Good-Friday dirges and doleful laments, God meets us on Sunday. Our eyes are closed. We are slow to see. We do not understand the words so God shows us, beckoning us to the table. There God takes bread, blesses it, breaks it, and gives it, and we *see*.

You can imagine how this Emmaus story challenges a traditional Protestant way of looking at worship. Protestants have always believed in the supremacy of the word—the word read, preached, studied, listened, and responded to. Sunday singing, praying, and other acts of worship seem mostly preliminaries to prepare for the sermon. Protestants have assumed whatever disclosure, recognition, and revelation there was to be had on Sunday would come this way, packaged and delivered from pulpit to pew.

As for the Lord's Supper and its bread and wine, well, that was permissible, but no more than once every three months and then preferably in the little chapel at 8:00 A.M. so as not to interfere with *real* worship (preaching) at 11:00 A.M. in the sanctuary.

The Emmaus story challenges this worship pattern.

At Emmaus, first the scriptures are opened. Then they are interpreted. But as is often the case with us—even in the speaking, hearing, teaching, and preaching—we do not always understand. We do not see the presence. Our Lord remains estranged from us. And so, as was often the case with Jesus, God not only spoke the word but he also *did* the word, moving from word to deed. The word became act at the table. The stranger became host. Then, at last their eyes were opened. Here we see a more ancient, more biblical pattern for Sunday gatherings of disciples than our present exclusive emphasis upon the sermon. In the meal, the word becomes flesh.

In the early church, the service of the word came first (scripture, psalms, and sermon). Then came the service of the table (the taking of the bread and wine, the prayer of thanksgiving or blessing, the breaking of the bread, the giving of the bread and cup). As at Emmaus, the church moved from reading and interpretation of the word to enactment of the word at the Lord's table.

This interplay of preaching and communion was the Sunday pattern of worship in the church for its first 1500 years and is still the Sunday pattern for the majority of the world's Christians. Those who see Sunday as a day for preaching alone are in the minority. The word alone is not enough. It was not enough at Emmaus when language was respected and Jesus himself did the preaching. It is certainly not enough today when talk is cheap and people are sinking in a mire of words. It is not a matter of the sermon being more or less important than the Lord's Supper. It is a matter of the two complementing one another. Word and table belong together.

We might think of it this way: A dozen red roses without the words, "I love you," are just a nice gesture. The words give meaning and direction to the gesture. Without the spoken word in scripture, prayer, and sermon (as well as the sung word in hymns, spirituals, and anthems), the meal is just a meal. The word claims the meal as communion. It sets our eating and drinking in context. As with Jesus' table talk at the meals in the gospels, so we contemporary disciples listen in on the conversation at the table and grow in our faith.

But without the meal, the word is not embodied and enacted. We rise, sing a hymn, and go home. We prepare to be with Jesus, the invitation is given, but we do not move to his table. The feast is laid before us but not enjoyed. We hear the call to faith and action but do not receive the nourishment of food and fellowship which sustains us on the way to faith and action. We cheat ourselves of the full experience of being with Christ.

The pastor's sermon is most helpful as a bold, pointed, contemporary interpretation and application of scripture to your life in this faith—a placing of the Bible alongside today's newspaper and a reading of the two together. The sermon reminds the church of its mandate and calls us to action. Therefore, the sermon is often a painful reminder that (in the words of a traditional prayer of confession): "We have erred and strayed from thy ways like lost sheep. We have followed too much the devices and desires of our hearts. We have offended against thy holy laws."

Then, after the sermon, when we are invited to the table, we move from lamentation of our misdeeds to celebration of God's deeds in Jesus Christ. We move beyond the contemporary to the future. We see beyond the present moment with its heartaches and tragedies and catch a vision of the future which God is building.

Without the meal, our worship can degenerate into sermonic scolding or weekly reiteration of our infidelities or constant cataloging of all the things we are not. (Alas, this is how sermons sound to many Christians: "Ten Reasons You Are *Not* a Christian.") But without the sermon, our communion can degenerate into giddy-headed, smiling, insensitive, "Smile-God-Loves-You" celebrations of our own fantasies about the world rather than a view of the way the world really is. The sermon keeps us rooted firmly in the now; the Lord's Supper opens our eyes to a vision of the now and the not yet. And as the prophet knew, where there is no vision, there is no hope. Where there is no hope, there is no good news. Where there is no good news, the people starve. They perish.

The worship pattern of the earliest Christians was one of word and table:

> They devoted themselves to the apostles' teaching and fellowship, to the breaking of bread and the prayers.
>
> —Acts 2:42

I grieve that our Sunday services seem more like memorials of God's absence rather than celebrations of God's presence. Our Sundays seem more like the gloom of Good Friday defeat than the joy of Easter victory.

The great weakness of our older services of Holy Communion (which we inherited from the Reformation) is that they never got us off our knees. The whole service was a tireless reiteration of all the reasons that nothing has changed in our world. Like the disciples on the way to Emmaus we ask, "What can anybody do?" We confess; we grovel; we complain. We come to the Lord's Table on our knees:

> We do not presume to come to this thy table, O merciful Lord, trusting in our own righteousness, but in thy manifold and great mercies. We are not worthy so much as to gather up the crumbs under thy table. But thou art the same Lord, whose property is always to have mercy.

Fortunately, the new services of the Lord's Supper move us from this Maundy Thursday-Good Friday gloom to Easter light. While not denying our sin, our infidelity, our weakness, they affirm God's work. Something *has* changed. The battle *has* been fought and won. True, there is still some major mopping-up work to be done in our lives and in the world—the daily skirmishes we fight with sin and death. But the war has been won.

A prayer of thanksgiving used in one denomination sets a joyous tone for the service:

> Father, it is right that we should always
> and everywhere give you thanks and praise.
>
> Only you are God.
> You created all things and called them good.
> You made us in your own image.
> Even though we rebelled against your love,
> you did not desert us.
> You delivered us from captivity,
> made covenant to be our Sovereign God,
> and spoke to us through your prophets.
>
> Therefore, we join the entire company of heaven
> and all your people now on earth
> in worshiping and glorifying you.[1]

If the church had intended to reenact the Last Supper and focus only upon the defeat and gloom of the cross, the church would have had communion once a year at Maundy Thursday.

Christians gathered on Sunday. Life being what it is—with all the injustice, pain, suffering, and death—it is easy to forget why they gathered. It is easy to throw up our hands and throw in the towel, to respond to today's sermon with a deep sigh and say, "But what can anybody do?"

Christians still gather on Sunday in order not to forget, in order to remember who we are and the victory which is ours in Jesus Christ. There, in the sermon and at the table, our eyes are opened and we see. We rise from the table, rushing out the door and into the world with the astounding news: "He is risen."

Many churches are reviving the ancient practice of standing for communion rather than kneeling. Thus our bodily posture reflects our spiritual stance. When we come into the presence of our Lord, our penitence becomes joy, our eyes are once again opened to the victory. So we stand with eyes open and hands outstretched to receive the victory which is ours in Jesus Christ.

In this life, we receive only fleeting, momentary glimpses of this joy: a kind word, a touch, a good deed here and there, a song along the way. So we come to the table, we watch as bread is blessed and broken, and we see. The joyful strain thunders forth, what has before been only a glimpse becomes a vision. We see.

We are forever pushing Jesus into some dim, distant, dusty past. We make him into a nice man who once lived, once taught, once died some place other than here, at some time other than now, among people other than ourselves.

"It was good while he was here," we say. "But alas, he has left us. Gone, but not forgotten." We do this to keep the whole Jesus story neat, removed, abstract, antique.

The amazing proclamation of this Sunday resurrection meal is that we need not impatiently wait until some distant future when Christ will return out of some distant past. We need not cool our heels in a 2000-year interim between his first and second comings. The old cop out, "But what can anybody do?" doesn't work anymore. This Lord will not let us off that easily.

Running from Emmaus, breathlessly breaking into Jerusalem, the two disciples made a peculiarly Easterlike declaration: He's back! Tombs cannot contain him, even the tombs we build which try to tuck him away in our dusty history, in our pessimistic defeatism, in our puny notions of what can and cannot be done.

Keeping at It

When we approach the truth, we approach the person of Jesus Christ. Christianity is not an idea, a concept, or a philosophy. It is basically a matter of being with Christ. For us, the truth is a person—personal. "*I am the way, and the truth, and the life,*" said Jesus (John 14:6a).

Therefore to be a Christian is not to think long thoughts about noble ideas. To be a Christian is to encounter a person. Faith comes in meeting, in spoken and unspoken dialogue, in a relationship with another who is close to you but also distant and mysterious.

Therefore we must understand Christ the way we understand a person: by spending time with the person; by being respectful and attentive; and by receiving what the person wishes to share, knowing that no matter how well we get to know the person, we cannot possess or control the person. To be with a friend, Jesus or any other, is to be patient and let that friend disclose himself or herself to us in his or her own good time.

Flagon and Loaf—Contemporary
Perkins School of Theology

You cannot rush relationships. If you try to force or prod the friend, friendship degenerates into manipulation in which we are using someone rather than enjoying someone. To be in friendship, to enter into the deep, unfathomable reality of another, is to be open to surprises, to risk being swept out of one's petty, selfish preoccupations into the joy of another's life. We must *stand under* this truth if we are to *understand* the truth as embodied in the person of Christ. This is how meeting happens. This is Communion.

And when we meet, when our beings are encountered by Christ's being, we are changed. No one can predict the results of such meeting and change, but we can be sure that we will not be the same. We leave the meeting changed, converted. And when such meeting and conversion happen at Communion, it's all the better. What better place to meet and risk change than at the table? It happens so much in everyday life, why not in church on Sunday?

You already know, in your encounters with persons, that friendship takes time. You must keep at it. You must be ready for long morning coffee breaks, leisurely lunches, times to put down your work and listen, late night telephone calls, and afternoons spent walking along the beach. Friends take time. This puts the frequently asked question, "How often should our church have the Lord's Supper?" into proper perspective. Remember, we are talking about growing in a relationship; we are talking about meeting; we are discussing nourishment.

Some justify infrequent Communion by saying that more frequent celebrations would become routine, that Communion would lose its significance. Unfortunately, 500 years of experience in churches which followed that line of thinking suggest that this point of view is wrong. Those churches which have Communion most often seem to value it most.

Quarterly celebrations of Holy Communion mean that pastor and people never get a chance to become accustomed to the ritual, to relax and be comfortable with the service. When they have the Lord's Supper, it feels strange to them, abnormal rather than special. But as we have said earlier, the Lord's Supper is not special: this meal is the normal, standard, Sunday morning activity for Christians. John Wesley, founder of Methodism, advocated weekly Communion; Wesley himself took Communion as often as three times a week.

How often should our church have the Lord's Supper? We might better ask, How often should we eat? We usually eat three meals a day. Admittedly, not all of our daily meals are special or full of significance. Some are, some are not. But that is not the point. We eat regularly, even routinely, ritualistically, because we need these gifts to live. The Lord's Supper is the normal food for Christians. Sometimes the service is special and significant for us. Sometimes it is not. But whether a service strikes you as deeply moving or as routine, the important thing is that you are fed.

We might respond to the question, How often should our church have the Lord's Supper? by asking, How often should we commune with the risen Christ? Is once every three months enough? Hardly. Friendship takes time, commitment, risk, frequent meetings. The more you get together, the more you grow together. Sometimes your gathering with a friend will be invigorating, inspiring, and full of significance. Sometimes it will be a cup of coffee, a little idle talk, and nothing more. But the important thing was that you met. You got together. You provided the opportunity for a deep encounter. You took time.

There is nothing wrong with routine. As long as you are doing something worthwhile, the routineness of your activity does not matter. I suppose most of us go to church out of habit. We also eat, sleep, hug our children, give to our favorite charity, make love, and a host of other life-giving acts out of habit. So what's wrong with good habits?

One reason that baptized children belong to the Lord's table is that they also need to keep at it. From our youngest years, we start forming the habits of discipleship. From our first sputtering emergence from the baptismal font, we start learning to confess, forgive, reach out, face the truth, be converted, be fed.

When our children were very young, I had the bright idea of feeding them an early supper and rushing them off to bed so my wife and I could sit down to a civilized, leisurely, quiet, uninterrupted meal later in the evening.

"No," my wife said. "How will they learn to eat at the table if they don't get a chance to practice, if they don't get to watch us?"

She was right. And what she says about family meals goes for the Lord's meal too. If we are going to grow and mature in our relationship with Christ, if we are to meet this Truth as he must be met, then all of us must keep at it on a regular basis. A lifelong series of big and little, significant and commonplace rhythm of meetings at the meal is required.

Easter Dinner

I confess to dry, dusty deserts in my own spiritual journey. I know the long stretches through illness, defeat, despair, boredom. My Maundy

Thursdays and Good Fridays come around more often than my Easter Sundays. After all, I read the papers. I listen to the six-o'clock news. I know that the good get it in the end. I tell myself: You can't fight city hall. What can anybody do?

Let us hold hands and think positively or else sing sad songs and catalogue our sins. Let us huddle close together in the cold dark night and keep each other warm. What can anybody do?

Then comes Sunday. As usual, the toast is burned, there is a soggy newspaper and you are out of toothpaste again. A glimpse in the mirror reveals that you are not getting any younger and the lump on the back of your neck is larger. The kids are scolded and are dressed at last. You pile them into the car and silently drive to church past all your neighbors who are again sitting Sunday out. It is the same crowd at church: same small numbers, same hymns, same preacher, same words. Your eyes grow heavy with boredom and you struggle to keep consciousness amid the typical and the expected.

Then the invitation is given. Your neighbor reaches out and places bread in your empty hands. You smell the cup. You taste the bread. You eat. You drink. Eyes flash open. Morning sunlight streams in upon you. You feel fed. Full. *You see.*

And once again, for you as it was for the early Christians, your eyes open. Maundy Thursday becomes Easter Sunday. The bridegroom has arrived. The party has begun. Resurrection occurs. And like the others before you, you rise, bounding past the bolted-down pews, rushing out the door, running all the way back into the world, shouting, *"He is risen!"*

> Day by day, attending the temple together and breaking bread in their homes, they partook of food with glad and generous hearts.
> —Acts 2:46

CHAPTER TEN

Let's Get Together

Because there is one loaf, we who are many are one body, for we all partake of the one loaf.
— 1 Corinthians 10:17

Eating Together

As usual, I was busy. There were letters to be written and next Sunday's bulletin to be done and another hospital to visit.

"I can make a quick call before lunch," I thought to myself. So I turned the car down the street where Mrs. Smith lives. Mrs. Smith has lived alone "since the war" when her husband died. Her little white house sits surrounded by trees, two bird feeders, and a vintage-era, black Dodge.

My quick visit to Mrs. Smith was not to be. Once in her living room, seated in a rose-colored armchair, I was told by this tiny woman, "You'll be staying for lunch." I protested, listing all the things I had to do. "You are too busy," she responded. "Everyone has to eat. I'll get the table ready." And that was that.

"Please don't go to any trouble for me," I said, settling back in the chair, realizing that I was here for the duration of lunch, busy or not. Out of an oak buffet came an ancient linen tablecloth, looking as if it had been folded there since time began.

"Be sure not to go to any trouble for me," I asked.

Mrs. Smith continued, oblivious to my protests. The ritual of preparation had begun, and she was not to be diverted by my irrelevant chatter. Her attention was fixed now upon the china cabinet. Crystal glasses were lovingly taken in hand; rich, Irish, cut glass—gift of her wedding day, I thought. Then the plates, platters, butter dish, and vessels were ready.

"I really wish you wouldn't bother yourself. I'm on my way back to the office anyway and I. . . ."

"You'll have to stop talking," she said, "I'm going to be in the kitchen for a few minutes. You amuse yourself in here. And don't follow me into the kitchen. I don't like people staring at me when I'm cooking gravy."

Again I settled back in the rose-colored chair as she disappeared into the holy of holies to concoct the meal. I would not witness those mysteries today. But I could smell the biscuits rising to a golden brown, the ham sizzling in the pan. I could hear the ice cubes tinkling into the glasses. And I waited, contenting myself by looking around her living room of faded pastels and browning pictures of "Mr. Smith," as she called him; a tattered, old Bible rested on the coffee table, not for show but for daily use.

The priestess burst forth from the kitchen with dishes steaming like incense and announced, "Come to the table."

I was seated in a large oak chair with arms—"Mr. Smith's chair," she said. I was then told to "give thanks." I did and we began. After a few wonderful mouthfuls of food and a few inane comments by me about how good everything was, she said to me, "Preacher, perhaps you forgot how difficult it is to eat alone. I never feel alone in my house, except at mealtimes. Mr. Smith said when we invited company for dinner—which we did nearly every other night—'The Lord never intended us to eat by ourselves.' "

Eating Alone

We got our recent custom of using individual glasses at Communion from Scotch Presbyterians and others who, in order to recover the meal at the Lord's Supper, gave each communicant a glass of wine and a small bun, seated the congregation at tables, and had a meal which looked and tasted like a meal. The custom of using individual, pressed, white, tasteless wafers is an extension of medieval preoccupations with the bread as a holy, untouched, spotless portion of Christ's body. Over the years, both the glasses and the wafers got smaller until the church seemed to be having a make-believe meal without food. We know now that from the beginning it was not so.

Add to these developments early twentieth-century preoccupations with and myths about germs, and you have communion as it is "celebrated" in many churches today: self-contained, thimble-size glasses and tasteless, infinitesimal bits of bread far removed from the original, biblical experience of eating with Jesus, now almost incomprehensible to the average person.

I finally said "enough is enough" a couple of years ago when I read of a man in the West who, believing that the Lord's Supper is time consuming and cumbersome because of the individual cups involved, has begun marketing a product for those in a hurry.

He produces airtight packets which contain a crackerlike pellet in one compartment and two grams of grape juice in another compartment —a disposable, self-contained, eat-on-the-run Lord's Supper—sort of, "This is my body packaged for you."

There you have it. The last hindrance to totally self-contained, self-centered religion is removed. We have drive-in churches, Dial-a-Prayer, offering by mail, and TV preachers, so why not self-contained communion? Now, thanks to this unit packaging, we need never come into contact with or be touched by another human being again. Just when you thought that modern life had depersonalized the gospel to the utmost, we have another breakthrough—Communion without communion!

The rugged individualism and the self-made-man mentality in the United States have led to a vast heresy which speaks of religion as a private affair. Communion and community are forsaken for the so-called electronic church—a "church" where everyone stays at home and does his or her own thing without the bother of other people. Mainline churches split into a plethora of caucus groups, special interest cliques, clergy-versus-laity battles, and feuding factions.

Where the society at large is concerned, the generation gap, the separation of the races, and the growing distance between rich and poor all testify to a people in pursuit of loneliness. Isolated, cut off, walled in behind our armed security guards and fences, encased in our cocoons of navel-gazing inwardness and self-pitying solitude, it is little wonder that we should seek a TV religion which has all the convenience, loneliness, self-centeredness, and tastelessness of a TV dinner.

A leader of the California tax revolt voices our new credo, "It's them or us and we're for us." More accurately, it's me or them and I'm for *me*.

I thought about the problems at First Church Corinth. We discussed the Corinthian factionalism in chapters four and eight of this book. The Corinthians were bitterly divided (1 Cor. 1:1-12). Even the gifts of the Spirit were a source of division rather than unity (1 Cor. 12). Paul, in First Corinthians 11:17-34, turns to the Lord's Supper as a means of healing the Corinthians' brokenness.

Paul contrasts the table of the Lord with what he calls the "table of demons" (10:21). The church's divisions have corrupted the sacred meal. Some eat and drink to drunkenness while others starve. "When you meet together, it is not the Lord's Supper that you eat," (11:20), Paul tells them. In their failure to realize the common life, they fail to "discern the body" (v. 29). The "body" here is the church, the "Body of Christ." (See Rom. 12.) At the Lord's Supper, each person eats for himself or herself, thus defiling the unity which the church seeks. The Corinthians eat a selfish *idion diepnon* (meaning "your own meal"), rather than the communal *kurakan diepnon* ("Lord's Supper"). Their selfish meals are a blasphemous mockery of the communion which the Lord's Supper is meant to be.

How interesting that Paul's test for the validity of our worship is not the qualifications of the celebrant, correct formulae, proper rubrics, or other liturgical tests we often apply! The test is in the quality of the community's life together. Contrast Paul's view of worship with that held by many today. Many people see Sunday morning as primarily a private time for "me-and-Jesus" individualism and subjectivism. Individuals come and sit in individual pews and think individual thoughts and eat individual bread. We complain that the rumble of the children or the volume of the organ or the whispers of someone next to us interrupts our personal meditation.

Private, personal meetings with God have their time and place. But church on Sunday is not the time or the place. Sunday is family day. It is a joyous day to get together, to reform and re-form the body, to meet one another, and to meet God. We are called forth from our rugged individualism and yoked to the Body. Unlikely, separated individuals are converted into family. We come to the table as virtual strangers; we rise and go forth as kinfolk.

Sunday worship is corporate worship, corporate and corporeal. It forms the Body. Some churches are victims of worship which fosters private emotionalism; some are victims of private rationalism. Both are missing the point of Sunday. On Sunday, we come together not as a conglomeration of individuals, but as a body to pray with one heart and one voice.

As John Wesley said, "Christianity is a social religion; to turn it into a

Altar Table
All Saints Church
Basel, Switzerland

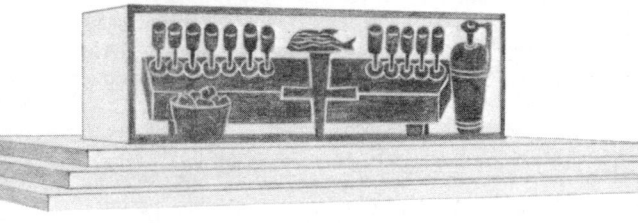

solitary thing is to destroy it." Or, as Wesley might have said, "Singing alone in the shower is fine as far as it goes, but nothing beats joining 200 other voices in the 'Hallelujah Chorus.' "

Solitary worshippers with eyes glued to individual bulletins, singing from individual hymnals, eating individual wafers and sipping from individual glasses are a poor image of what God wants to do for us on Sunday. Like the Corinthians, "each one goes ahead with his own meal" (11:21).

When I think of the sad brokenness of modern life, the tragic, lonely detachment we suffer, I can think of no more expressive symbol of this detachment than a miserly, plastic, disposable thimble of a glass in which watered-down, antiseptic juice is offered to God's thirsty people.

Eating Together

You have heard it said, "The family that prays together stays together." I say to you, "The family that *eats* together stays together." Could the breakdown of many of our families today be attributable, in part, to our failure to eat together? If the American family survives the TV dinner, it may not survive the microwave oven. Junior comes in from school, pops his hot dog in the microwave. Five minutes later, he is off to basketball practice. Then Sis arrives from ballet, unwraps her sandwich, flips the switch, and is off to the library in a flash. Mom comes home from work, opens a can of soup, puts it into the microwave, eats, and is off to the shopping mall. Dad will be home later for his minute-meal of frozen entree and a solitary evening snooze before the television.

Is it any wonder that our families are in trouble—strangers in a lonely, eat-and-run wilderness?

What is said of our human families can be said of the family of God as well: The disintegration of table fellowship often leads to the dissolution of the family. People who observe churches note that churches which enjoy a high level of fellowship, vitality, service, friendliness, and growth invariably spend much of their time at the table. The bigger and more widespread a church's membership, the more often it needs to eat together. After all, we know what happens to people who eat together.

This makes it doubly unfortunate that many of our larger congregations have Communion so infrequently. Larger churches sometimes claim that Communion is difficult for them because they have so many people to serve or it takes too long. If a church is too big to serve people, too big for people to fellowship with one another and with Christ on a regular basis, a church is too big to be a church! In order to have more frequent Communion, larger congregations may need to make adjustments in the way they serve Communion. There is no congregation where the service, including sermon, need necessarily take longer than an hour. Often, the things that take the most time are the nonessentials: repetitious table dismissals, unduly detailed instructions, too many musical selections, a prolonged sermon, too few servers.

People can be invited to the table with a simple, "Come to the Lord's table." They do not need detailed information or overly regimented ushers to get them from their seats to the communion rail. Save the hymns for the time during the Communion when people come forward. The entire congregation should be singing the communion hymns, not the choir alone. People can come to and go from the table without lengthy directions and dismissals; they do not need to come or to be dismissed row by row. It is odd that many of us in large churches claim that we are too big for Communion when some of the largest churches in the country are of denominations which have Communion every Sunday. Lay servers can assist the pastor in distributing the elements. Lay assistance in serving Communion can be a beautiful sign of the ministry of the laity. It can also facilitate Communion without making it seem impersonal or rushed.

Any method or activity which makes Communion impersonal and regimented must be changed. We will not form the Body of Christ at Communion if we treat the faithful like cattle or robots. One large loaf and one large cup are good symbols of the unity we share in Christ. The bread should be placed in people's hands, while the server looks the recipient in the eyes and, if possible, calls the person's Christian name: "John, the Body of Christ, given for you." If people are concerned about hygiene, the pieces of bread can be dipped into the chalice (the so-called intinction method). This is an ancient practice which allows us to use a common loaf and a common cup without actually drinking from the same cup.

In Communion, in partaking of the same cup and the same loaf, we act out what we would like to be as a church; we practice eating as the Body of Christ so that we might become the Body of Christ. "Because there is one loaf, we who are many are one body, for we all partake of the same loaf," Paul told the Corinthians (1 Cor. 10:17). In other words, when we remember Christ in this meal, we "re-member" the Body of Christ. We get this painfully disjointed Body back together. One of the earliest Christian prayers spoke of how, just as one loaf of bread is made from many individual grains of wheat, so the one church is made from many individual followers of Christ. This, then, is the mystery of those who partake of the same bread and who follow the same Lord.

From the earliest days, the Lord's Supper was seen as a reconciliation meal. Just as state banquets ratify a treaty between two nations, so the Lord's Supper ratifies and recognizes our reconciliation, our reunion with God. This is the meal of the new testament, the new covenant which Christ has sealed.

This reconciliation between God and humanity provides the setting whereby humanity can be reconciled to itself. In the early church, after the prayers and before the offering, Christians joined in an embrace which they called "the peace." This bodily gesture of reconciliation and love acts out Christ's admonition, "If you are offering your gift at the altar, and there remember that your brother has something against you, leave your gift there before the altar and go; first be reconciled to your brother, and then come and offer your gift" (Matt. 5:23-24). The peace, which is being recovered and celebrated today in our new liturgies for the Lord's Supper, is one more way in which we act out with our bodies in worship what we feel in our hearts.

For if there is a corporate aspect to sin, then there must also be a corporate response to it. Most of us are better as individuals than we are in groups. The power of the mob mentality is strong. Our human weakness to follow the crowd, to merge into the herd, to join others in doing wrong simply because "everyone else is doing it" testifies to our corporate sin. Our racism, sexism, and all our other "isms" are evidence of our corporate participation in evil.

Corporate sin needs corporate response. That is why at the beginning of many of our services of worship we join in a corporate prayer of confession. Sometimes it may seem odd to you to be confessing sins from a printed page. After all, you may say, how do they know that these are *my* sins? But haven't we learned, in the tragic events of the late twentieth century, that the rest of the problem is *our* sin—our shared human capacity to join the mob in its nameless, faceless, anonymous evil?

And so we have the church's corporate fellowship as we struggle with the sin about us. The Body of Christ is that whole fellowship who struggle with sin and death, not a conglomeration of isolated believers. Together we grow. Together we admonish one another, we enable one another to minister, we accomplish as a group what we could never do as mere individuals. The grace we receive in Holy Communion is not some magical substance which we ingest like vitamins (as Paul, in effect, told the Corinthians). Grace comes in relationship with God, with God's creation, and with God's creatures.

It is only in Communion, in community, in God's community, that we get the support, vision, encouragement, discipline, forgiveness, rebirth, conversion, and nurture we need to be faithful followers of Christ. In the Body, we "bear one another's burdens" (Gal. 6:2). The grace of God is not often known by isolated individuals. In the beginning, the words thunder forth that our Creator has made us to be social creatures: "It is not good that the man should be alone" (Gen. 2:18a). Trying to go it alone is often our sinful attempt at self-sufficiency, denying our dependence upon one another.

What a perfect symbol of this *koinonia,* this communion, is Holy Communion. Bread and wine are gifts of God, yes. But they are also products of corporate human labor, now more than ever. Think of all the hands that put bread upon your table this morning. When someone hands you bread at communion, when someone shares it with you, at that moment, at that mysterious, deep moment, you encounter, in a moment, the very heart of the gospel mystery: It is not good to be alone, therefore God brings us together. Where two or three are gathered, there our Lord is also.

Let's get together sometime. The table is spread; all is now ready. The church points you to the table, the Lord's Table, and says: There is no better time to get together than now; there is no better place than here.

And you come. As you come, hear these words of Saint Augustine, spoken on a Sunday long ago as he invited his flock to the Lord's Table:

> The apostles explain the meaning of this bread to us with the words: "We who are many are *one* bread, *one* body." (I Corinthians 10:17) O sacrament of love! O sign of unity! . . . Whoever seeks life can find a source of life here. Let him come forward and let himself be incorporated, and he will be given life. Let him not shrink back from the binding of the members to one another. . . . Let him hold on firmly to the body.[1]

> *"They said to him, 'Lord, give us this bread always' " (John 6:34). And so he does.*

Notes

Chapter 1
1. The following description of an early celebration of the Lord's Supper is reconstructed from Justin Martyr's account of about A.D. 155. See Bard Thompson, ed., *Liturgies of the Western Church* (New York: World Publishing Co., 1961), pp. 3-7.

Chapter 2
1. William Temple, *Nature, Man and God* (London: Macmillan and Co., 1964), p. 478.
2. I am indebted to Edward Schillebeeckx's *Christ: The Sacrament of the Encounter with God* (New York: Sheed and Ward, 1968) for the substance of these thoughts on the real presence.
3. "Constitution on the Sacred Liturgy," *The Documents of Vatican II*, ed. Walter M. Abbott, S. J. (New York: Corpus Books, 1966), pp. 140-41.

Chapter 4
1. Karl Barth, *The Christian Life*, trans. Geoffrey W. Bromiley (Grand Rapids, Michigan: William B. Eerdmans Publishing Co., 1981), p. 80.

Chapter 6
1. I am grateful for the research done by Theodore Runyon on John Wesley for his article, "Will You Recommend Fasting or Abstinence?" appearing in *Ministry & Mission*, vol. 2, no. 4 (Dec. 1977), p. 2, and am deeply indebted to that article.

Chapter 9
1. *We Gather Together*, Supplemental Worship Resources 10 (Nashville: The United Methodist Publishing House, 1980), p. 8.

Chapter 10
1. Quoted by Bernard Häring, *A Sacramental Spirituality*, trans. R. A. Wilson (New York: Sheed and Ward, 1965), p. 152.

An Educational Introduction

Sunday Dinner: The Lord's Supper and the Christian Life is a natural continuation of *Remember Who You Are: Baptism, A Model for Christian Life.* William Willimon has once again penned a readable, theologically sound, stimulating book for persons who want to understand the Lord's Supper and make it more meaningful in their church's life. From the beginning of the church, Christians gathered on each Sunday, "the Lord's Day," and ate a meal of great religious significance —the Lord's Supper. While Christians today call this event by different names—Eucharist, Holy Communion, Mass, or Lord's Supper—most Protestant and Roman Catholic theologicans have reached consensus on the nature and character of this central act in the life of the Christian church. First, they have agreed that both *the biblical and the historical records set as the norm for Christians a weekly celebration of word and table which moves from the celebration and proclamation of the Scrip tures to participation in the Lord's Supper.* To gather for Sunday worship and fail to climax that worship with the celebration of Holy Communion or to ignore the reading of scripture with sermon is to have cheated oneself of the full experience of Christian worship on the Lord's Day.

Second, *the Lord's Supper or Eucharist is primarily a corporate and communal act of worship.* It is an occasion for community and communion rather than a time for a personal, private meeting with God. In that regard, the Lord's Supper is understood as a family meal; therefore all baptized Christians of whatever age are invited to the Lord's Table. I agree with Dr. Willimon that it is utterly inconsistent to baptize children without communing them.

Third, *the Lord's Supper or Eucharist reminds us that Christianity is a "materialistic" faith.* The ordinary, familiar, basic stuff of everyday life—bread and wine—opens up new levels of communion with the Divine in our midst. All of our senses are engaged in this multi-media, sensuous, multi-faceted experience of the divine-human encounter. For too long, many of us have been in the grip of a passive, non-participatory, heady, rational understanding of the faith. The Lord's Supper can lead us back to a more participative, engaging experience of God.

Fourth, there is agreement that *the Lord's Supper has a victorious redemptive focus more than a somber, funereal, penitential one.* The early Christians celebrated their sacred meal on Sunday—the Lord's Day, the day of victorious resurrection. Those who gathered around The Lord's Table might have been sinners, but they were *redeemed* sinners. Many of us have inherited a heavily sin-obsessed penitential understanding of the Lord's Supper that prevents celebration and joy in the Christian gospel. While it is appropriate to have such a somber expression during a season such as Lent, it is important to realize that we are indeed a redeemed people and that we have much to celebrate and be thankful for.

Fifth, *the Lord's Supper or Eucharist is an "Apostolic" event.* The goal of our Communion, our fellowship, our proclamation and the celebration of our redemption is witness in the world. To go to the Lord's Table is not to escape or to experience simply warm-hearted togetherness. Our goal is to find ourselves offered, blessed, and broken at the Lord's Table so that, being fed and nourished, we may be strengthened and commissioned for life in the world. Communion is an evangelistic, missional activity which equips us for radical service and witness to the world outside the confines of our table fellowship.

While these contentions are commonly known and accepted by theologians, few lay persons have had an opportunity to understand and reflect upon them. Indeed, such contentions may appear radical and strange. Most Protestants experience the Lord's Supper as an event held a few times a year in a service dominated by an individualistic, somber, penitential mode in which there is relatively little participation. While many have had significant religious experiences at such occasions, many stay away when the Lord's Supper is celebrated. Few realize that their personal experience and understanding of the Lord's Supper has a very short history. The agreements mentioned earlier are more typical of the church throughout its history.

Today almost every denomination or religious community is being introduced to changes in the nature of Sunday worship, changes that are consistent with the characteristics outlined above. Many persons are confused and need help to understand what is occurring. Dr. Willimon's book serves as an excellent introduction to those who are concerned about their life of worship in the Christian community of faith. I enthusiastically recommend its use as a teaching resource, and I am honored to have had the opportunity to prepare the educational guide to accompany it.

JOHN H. WESTERHOFF III
Duke University Divinity School
Maundy Thursday, 1981

An Educational Guide
for a Church School Class
or Adult Study Group

The chapters of this book are presented for easy use in a ten-week course for a group of adults. What follows is an educational guide. If you prefer, you can adapt the suggested exercises for individual use, either alone or with your pastor's guidance. If you have fewer than ten weeks it is possible to combine chapters to meet your needs.

Before your first class meeting, reflect on the most meaningful meal you can remember. Then write a description of that meal: who was present, what kind of food did you have, what did you do, and how did you feel about it?

After you have completed this exercise, read chapter one.

1. Memories of Meals

When you meet, share your descriptions of memorable meals. After each is read, note on newsprint any occurrences recalled which had to do with identity (celebrating who you are) and/or remembering (celebrating where you came from—your roots).

Now discuss the question: How do these experiences of memorable meals compare and/or contrast with your experiences of identity and remembering at the Lord's Supper?

Together, write a single paragraph story of who you are as a Christian and where you came from as it is told at each celebration of the Lord's Supper.

Preparation

In preparation for the next session, write a description of what you see when you look at the bread and the wine at communion. Also write a description of the feelings which you experience when you eat the bread and drink the wine.

After you have completed this exercise, read chapter two.

2. He Took Bread and Blessed It

Begin by sharing the descriptions you prepared for this session. Record them on newsprint, indicating where there is agreement and disagreement.

Ask everyone to indicate individually whether or not they believe that Christ is present in the eating of bread and the drinking of wine, or explain why they do or do not believe that is so. Then ask the question: What difference does it make in your life to believe that Christ is present at the Lord's Supper?

Preparation

In preparation for the next session, write a description of what you use in your church for bread (what it is and what it looks like) and what it is that you use for wine. Now write a defense or a criticism of the way you experience bread and wine in your communion service.

After you have completed this exercise, read chapter three.

3. Let the Party Begin

Begin by sharing the descriptions of the bread and wine used in your Lord's Supper and the defense/criticisms that were prepared for class. Note on newsprint where there is agreement or disagreement about the type of elements you use.

Now ask the groups to summarize as fairly as possible the position and its defenses found in chapter three of this book.

Strive to reach a group consensus on bread and wine for communion.

Does your experience of the Lord's Supper remind you of (1) a funeral, (2) a party, or (3) a retirement banquet? Why?

Preparation

In preparation for the next session, find three persons who always come to church when the Lord's Supper is celebrated and three persons who always stay away. Ask them if they would explain to you their reasons for coming or not coming. Record their responses.

After you have completed this exercise, read chapter four.

4. What's a Savior Like You Doing with Sinners Like Us?

Begin by sharing your interviews. Now ask people to explain why they come or stay away, when it is that they come and when it is that they stay away.

Now discuss: in what ways are our reasons and our interviewees' reasons for participating or not participating in the Lord's Supper related to this chapter's discussion on saints and sinners.

Who might feel unwanted or unworthy at your church's celebrations of the Lord's Supper? What could your church do to make them feel more welcome?

Preparation

In preparation for the next session, write a description of the persons who come to The Lord's Supper in your church. Be honest. Describe what they look like (whoever they are) their racial backgrounds, their ages, their physical characteristics, and their marital, educational, and economic situations. In what ways are they alike or different?

After you have completed this exercise, read chapter five.

5. When You Give a Party

Begin by making a chart on newsprint listing these characteristics:

Age:	children	youth	adults	aging
Economics:	extremely poor	poor	middle class	wealthy
Race:	white	black	yellow	brown
Health:	mentally retarded	emotionally ill	physically handicapped	generally healthy
Education:	illiterate	poorly educated	educated	well educated
Moral Life:	criminals	immoral	generally moral	exemplary

Now ask the group to indicate the number of persons that they have observed at your Lord's Table in each of the categories listed on the newsprint.

Discuss your findings in relationship to the position taken in chapter five. Does your church's "guest list" resemble that in the parable of the Great Banquet? Why or why not?

Preparation

In preparation for the next session, think about the hungriest you have ever been. Write a poem on the topic of "Hunger" or draw a picture on the theme of "Hunger."

After you have completed this exercise, read chapter six.

6. Blessed Are the Hungry

Begin by sharing your drawings and poems. Discuss what comes to mind when you hear "food for the body," "food for the mind," "food for the soul." Then discuss the relationship of these three foods and how they relate to your understandings of hunger. How does the Lord's Supper help meet these hungers?

Describe the understandings of hunger as presented in chapter six and then together prepare a bulletin insert for your church on "Hunger and the Lord's Supper."

Preparation

In preparation for the next session, secure from your minister a copy of your congregation's service of Holy Communion. Also secure a copy of We Gather Together *(Supplemental Worship Resource 10) and compare and contrast these two services in terms of the experience a person has or might have when participating in them.*

After you have completed this exercise, read chapter seven.

7. In the Upper Room

Begin by having your minister celebrate the Word and Table Service in *We Gather Together* for your class. In the light of this experience, share your presentation exercises. Discuss which service—the one you typically use at your church or the one in *We Gather Together*—comes closest to being "Good News" as discussed in chapter seven.

Preparation

In preparation for the next session, interview ten persons in your congregation. Ask them what they call the piece of furniture on which you celebrate the Lord's Supper and around which you gather for Holy Communion—a table or an altar? Then ask them why they prefer to name it as they do. After you have conducted this interview, read chapter eight.

8. Proclaiming Death

Begin by sharing the results of your interviews.

Now ask each person in your group to describe his or her image of the Jesus they meet at the Lord's Supper. Ask: How many of us described a gnarled, unattractive Jesus twisted in pain sacrificing his life for us in love on a cross? Or did we picture a kind host at a table? Discuss why we did or did not do so.

Ask the group to summarize as fairly as possible the argument in chapter eight. Discuss what significance it would make in our lives if we called our gathering point for Holy Communion an altar.

Visit your church's sanctuary. Look at it as if you were seeing it for the first time. What message does this room and its furnishings "proclaim"?

Preparation

In preparation for the next session, write a description of the most meaningful worship service you have ever attended. Also describe an occasion that you remember when you experienced the good news of the resurrection. Now read chapter nine.

9. When He Was at Table with Them

Begin by sharing your preparation exercises. Summarize as fairly as possible Dr. Willimon's argument that both a sermon based on scripture and the Lord's Supper should be the usual pattern for each Sunday. Discuss: How do you react to this contention in the light of your own experience and the witness of the Bible?

How can participation in the Lord's Supper help a person to better understand scripture and sermons?

Preparation

In preparation for the next session, write three descriptions of times when you experienced true community. Now read chapter ten.

10. Let's Get Together

Begin by sharing your descriptions of community. How many of you have experienced community at the Lord's Supper? How do your church's celebrations of the Lord's Supper help or hinder formation of community?

Summarize as fairly as possible the content of chapter ten. Ask: What could we do in our church so that persons might experience true community at the Lord's Supper?

Now that you have completed your course of study, together write a report for your minister explaining what you believe Sunday worship should look like in your congregation. Present that report to the minister.

Index of Scripture

Old Testament

New Testament

Subject Index